Stonehenge

New and future titles in the series include:

Alien Abductions

Angels

The Bermuda Triangle

The Curse of King Tut

Dragons

ESP

Extinction of the Dinosaurs

Haunted Houses

The Kennedy Assassinations

King Arthur

The Loch Ness Monster

Pyramids

Stonehenge

UFOs

Unicorns

Vampires

Witches

The Mystery Library

Stonehenge

William W. Lace

LUCENT
BOOKS®

THOMSON
──────✦──────
GALE

San Diego • Detroit • New York • San Francisco • Cleveland • New Haven, Conn. • Waterville, Maine • London • Munich

© 2003 by Lucent Books. Lucent Books is an imprint of The Gale Group, Inc.,
a division of Thomson Learning, Inc.

Lucent Books® and Thomson Learning™ are trademarks used herein under license.

For more information, contact
Lucent Books
27500 Drake Rd.
Farmington Hills, MI 48331-3535
Or you can visit our Internet site at http://www.gale.com

LIBRARY OF CONGRESS CATALOGING-IN-PUBLICATION DATA

Lace, William W.
    Stonehenge / by William W. Lace.
        p. cm. — (The mystery library)
Includes bibliographical references and index.
Summary: Discusses the mystery and theories surrounding the ancient stone structure in
Wiltshire, England, called Stonehenge, whose purpose has been puzzled over since at
least the twelfth century.
        ISBN 1-59018-131-X (hardback : alk. paper)
    1. Stonehenge (England) —Juvenile literature.   2. Wiltshire (England)—
Antiquities—Juvenile literature.   3. Megalithic monuments—England—Wiltshire—
Juvenile literature. [1. Stonehenge (England) 2. Megalithic monuments. 3. England—
Antiquities.] I. Title.   II. Mystery library (Lucent Books)
    DA142 .L33 2003
    936.23' 19—dc21
                                                                        2002152981

Printed in the United States of America

Contents

Foreword   6

Introduction   8
    The Puzzle on the Plain

Chapter One   11
    The Silent Stones

Chapter Two   25
    Merlin and Magic

Chapter Three   36
    Romans, Danes, and Phoenicians

Chapter Four   47
    Aubrey, Stukeley, and the Druids

Chapter Five   61
    The Archaeologists

Chapter Six   76
    The Astronomers

Chapter Seven   88
    New Age, New Druids, New
    Theories

Epilogue   100
    For Every Season

Notes   103
For Further Reading   106
Works Consulted   107
Index   108
Picture Credits   112
About the Author   112

Foreword

In Shakespeare's immortal play, *Hamlet*, the young Danish aristocrat Horatio has clearly been astonished and disconcerted by his encounter with a ghostlike apparition on the castle battlements. "There are more things in heaven and earth," his friend Hamlet assures him, "than are dreamt of in your philosophy."

Many people today would readily agree with Hamlet that the world and the vast universe surrounding it are teeming with wonders and oddities that remain largely outside the realm of present human knowledge or understanding. How did the universe begin? What caused the dinosaurs to become extinct? Was the lost continent of Atlantis a real place or merely legendary? Does a monstrous creature lurk beneath the surface of Scotland's Loch Ness? These are only a few of the intriguing questions that remain unanswered, despite the many great strides made by science in recent centuries.

Lucent Books' Mystery Library series is dedicated to exploring these and other perplexing, sometimes bizarre, and often disturbing or frightening wonders. Each volume in the series presents the best-known tales, incidents, and evidence surrounding the topic in question. Also included are the opinions and theories of scientists and other experts who have attempted to unravel and solve the ongoing mystery. And supplementing this information is a fulsome list of sources for further reading, providing the reader with the means to pursue the topic further.

The Mystery Library will satisfy every young reader's fascination for the unexplained. As one of history's greatest scientists, physicist Albert Einstein, put it:

> The most beautiful thing we can experience is the mysterious. It is the source of all true art and science. He to whom this emotion is a stranger, who can no longer wonder and stand rapt in awe, is as good as dead: his eyes are closed.

The Puzzle on the Plain

About 1130, sixty-four years after the Norman Conquest of England, the bishop of Lincoln directed one of his priests, Henry of Huntingdon, to write a history of the recently acquired kingdom. Henry included in his book a description of the country's wonders. Prominent was "Stonehenge, where stones of an amazing size are set up in the manner of doorways, so that one door seems to be set upon another. Nor can anyone guess by what means so many stones were raised so high, or why they were built there."[1]

Henry's is the first known reference to Stonehenge. He doubtless was not the first person to gaze on this stone circle, wondering who built it and for what purpose. Certainly, he was not the last. From that time to this, kings and statesmen, artists and authors, mystics and scientists, and millions of ordinary people have come to the lonely plain in southwest England where Stonehenge stands in silent solitude. All have had the same questions: Who built Stonehenge? When? How? Why?

The Question of "Why?"

Science has answered, to the satisfaction of most people, some of the questions surrounding Stonehenge. The greatest mystery of all, however, remains: Why was it built? What motive impelled an ancient civilization to expend the

effort to haul these gigantic stones great distances and set them up in this particular manner?

The mysteries of Stonehenge have been deep, and the clues for solving them have been slow to unravel. People throughout the ages, therefore, have had to rely on their imagination. Every age has brought new and more diverse theories—some merely guesswork—as to why the monument was built. Indeed, the passage of centuries and the increase of scientific knowledge about Stonehenge have done little to stem the growing tide of speculation.

The mysteries surrounding Stonehenge have remained mostly unsolved for many millennia.

Looking Within

The lack of solid facts has also meant that those who would interpret Stonehenge have looked both within and without for answers. They have tended to reflect their own experiences and prejudices in their attempts to explain the monument. As products of their various centuries, they have posed their theories according to the character of the

9

age. In a time when people believed in magic, Stonehenge was called the product of a magician. In the computer age, it became a computer.

Perhaps some day the last mystery of Stonehenge will be solved. Until that day, however, the curious will continue to come to the plain, gaze on the stones, and whisper, "What are you?" And Stonehenge will whisper back, "What do you want me to be?"

Chapter 1

The Silent Stones

The question surrounding many of the world's mysteries is extremely basic: Do they exist? Is there a monster in the depth of Scotland's Loch Ness? Does Bigfoot really roam the mountainous wilderness in the American West? Do unidentified flying objects have any basis in fact?

Such is not the case with Stonehenge, the mysterious stone circle on an English plain about seventy miles southwest of London. There is no fuzzy photo here, no ambiguous snippet of film or videotape. Stonehenge is as real and solid as the stones from which it is made.

The mystery of Stonehenge, rather, is not whether it exists, but why, when, and by whom it was built. Before exploring what might be, however, it is valuable—perhaps essential—to study what is: the physical reality of Stonehenge.

To begin to understand Stonehenge, one must examine it in the context of its surroundings—not just the grassy plain on which it stands, but the entire British Isles. Stonehenge is the most famous ancient site, but hardly the only one. The landscape of Western Europe is dotted with monuments that ancient peoples have erected. More than ten thousand of these monuments are in Britain alone.

Many of the ancient monuments are barrows, tombs covered with mounds of earth or stone. Wiltshire, the English county in which Stonehenge stands, has more than twenty-three hundred barrows. Some are small, but others cover multiple chambers holding dozens of bodies and can be more than one hundred yards long.

Megaliths

Megaliths, or "great stones," are another type of ancient monument. Many are the fairly small tomb markers called dolmen, commonly consisting of two upright stones on which a capstone has been placed. Other megaliths include the famous stone circles, of which Stonehenge is only one.

Stonehenge, in fact, is not even the largest stone circle in England. About twenty miles to the north is the village of Avebury, which is almost completely surrounded by a ditch about twelve hundred feet in diameter, inside of which is a circle of more than one hundred stones as large as those at Stonehenge.

Stonehenge, therefore, is surrounded by other mysterious sites that only deepen the mystery. Are the barrows the tombs of the builders of Stonehenge? Did the same people who built Avebury build Stonehenge? If so, was it earlier or

Pictured is the processional entrance to Avebury, England's largest stone circle.

later, and why are the sites so different? And what about the other megaliths throughout Britain and their possible relationship to Stonehenge?

Although surrounded by other ancient sites, Stonehenge has seized imaginations as has no other. Avebury, for instance, although much grander in scale, has never attracted the attention of its neighbor to the south. One reason may be that its vastness is hard to grasp, whereas Stonehenge is more compact and easier to visualize. In addition, the stones of Avebury are rough in comparison to those at Stonehenge, most of which obviously have been "dressed," or shaped by human hands.

One reason for Stonehenge's popularity might be as simple as its location, easily accessible from the major cathedral city of Salisbury just eight miles to the south. Most modern-day visitors follow the same route as those who came a thousand years before them—north to the town of Amesbury, then west another two miles.

The First View

The first view most people have of Stonehenge comes as they crest a small hill from the east. The road dips, then rises on the far side of a shallow valley. As the road rises, it forks—the left side leading to the town of Exeter, the right to Devises. Inside the fork, closer to the right-hand road and just below the top of the hill, lies Stonehenge.

The location does not appear to have been chosen for maximum visibility, as it would if it were on top of the hill. The hill is not especially prominent, but is much the same as many others around it. Indeed, it is unclear if visibility was at all a consideration, since the landscape could well have been primarily forest when Stonehenge was built.

Many people have found this first view of Stonehenge somewhat disappointing. Having read about the huge size of the megaliths, they expect something grander or more

Counting the Stones

One of the most popular legends about Stonehenge is that it is impossible to count the stones twice and come up with the same number. As Sir Philip Sidney wrote in the 1500s:

Neer Wilton sweet, huge heapes of
  stones are found
But so confus'd, that neither any eye
Can count them just, nor reason try
What force them brought to so
unlikely ground.

Furthermore, a guidebook in the 1700s said, "It was vulgarly said that whoever counts the stones of the Stonehenge will die." And Daniel Defoe, the author of *Robinson Crusoe,* in his 1690 book about a tour of the countryside, wrote, "A baker carry'd a basket of bread, and laid a loaf upon every stone, and yet could never make out the same number twice."

The reason for the confusion is that some people count each fragment as a stone, while others count as one stone one that has obviously broken into two or more pieces. Stonehenge probably had about 162 stones when it stood complete. Today, counting fragments that obviously belong together as a single stone, there are perhaps 72.

The quotations are found in *Stonehenge Complete* by Christopher Chippindale.

overwhelming than this huddle of stones in the middle of a vast, open plain. Indeed, the main circle—only about one hundred feet across—is dwarfed by its surroundings. It is only when one stands next to the stones—the largest of which is almost thirty feet long and weighs almost ninety thousand pounds—that the size of Stonehenge and the effort it took to construct it begin to be understood.

Stonehenge is now made up of 90 stones—at least that is the commonly accepted number—mostly shaped into roughly rectangular form. In former years, experts disagreed on the number. Was it clear, for instance, that two adjacent pieces were parts of a single, broken stone? If so, should they be counted as two or one? When the monument was completed and whole, the number was around 162.

At the Center

The middle of Stonehenge is as good a place as any to begin a survey. The central stone, as were a few others, was given a fanciful name in the past, in this case the Altar Stone. The name was given when Stonehenge was widely thought to be some sort of temple, and the stone, lying as it does in the exact center, naturally reminded onlookers of an altar.

The sixteen-foot-long Altar Stone is unlike any other in the monument—a pale green sandstone with chips of mica that glisten in the sunlight. Where it came from, why the builders selected this one stone different from all others, and whether it was ever an altar are only three of the many mysteries that faced the early investigators of Stonehenge. And, if indeed it was an altar, who or what was worshiped there? When? By whom?

Surrounding the Altar Stone are five magnificent trilithons in the shape of a horseshoe. The word *trilithon*, combining the Greek words for "three" and "stones," refers to a pair of large upright stones, each shaped like a huge elongated brick. They are separated by a narrow space and covered with a lintel, or capstone, stretching across the tops of both uprights and the open space. The Anglo-Saxons, who ruled England for more than five hundred years before the Norman invasion, viewed the arrangement of uprights and lintels and used their words "stan" (stone) and either "hencg" (hinge) or "hen(c)en" (gallows) to give Stonehenge its name.

Mortises and Tenons

The lintels are secured by a system used more in carpentry than stonework, whereby a mortise, a hollowed-out space on the underside of the lintel, fits snugly onto a tenon—a protuberance on the top of the upright. As with all Stonehenge, no mortar was used.

When Stonehenge was completed, five trilithons were arranged in a horseshoe shape about forty-five feet across, the open end pointing northeast. The central trilithon (Great Trilithon) was the tallest at twenty-four feet (counting the lintel), and the others were progressively shorter toward the ends of the horseshoe. The stones in each trilithon were not the same length, but were placed in their holes at different depths so that equal parts were above ground. The uprights of the Great Trilithon, for instance, were thirty and twenty-six feet long, respectively, but eight feet of one and four feet of the other were placed belowground to make the tops even.

Only three of the five trilithons are intact today—the pair inside both ends of the horseshoe and the smaller outside trilithon on the east side. One upright remains on each of the other two. The other uprights and the lintels fell sometime in the distant past.

An Early Description

Dutchman Lucas de Heere visited England in the 1560s and later wrote a book about his travels. Included was one of the earliest detailed descriptions of Stonehenge. It is found in *Stonehenge Complete* by Christopher Chippindale.

These mentioned stones are massive [and] undressed [unfinished], from hard coarse material, of grey colour. They are generally about 18 or 20 feet high and about 8 feet wide over all four sides (for they are square). They stand two by two, each couple having one stone across, like a gallows, which stone has two mortises catching two stone tenons of the two upright stones. There seem to have been three ranks of stones, the largest of which comprises about three hundred feet in compass. But they are mostly decayed. One finds here-about many small hillocks or monticules, under which are sometimes found giants' bones (of which I possess one from which it can easily be perceived that the giant was as much as 12 feet tall, like there are also in London and elsewhere which are longer) and pieces of armour from captains which have been buried there.

Sarcen Stone

The trilithons are made of a sandstone called sarcen. In 1644 Richard Symonds, an army colonel passing through the vicinity of Stonehenge, wrote of "grey pibbles stone of great bigness . . . the inhabitants calling them Saracens' stones."[2] Saracen was a term that crusaders applied to their enemies in the Middle East. The huge stones, therefore, must have seemed so out of place that local people gave them their ultimate word for foreigner.

Even more foreign are the bluestones, which are arranged in a horseshoe shape just inside the trilithons, around the Altar Stone. The name comes from the bluish color of the stones, which are dolomite, a stone found nowhere near Stonehenge. Where did they come from, then? How and why were they brought to the site?

At one time, the horseshoe had nineteen bluestones, spaced about six feet apart. Only six remain upright, and three others survive only as short stumps. Two more have fallen, and the rest have disappeared. Since the bluestones are much smaller—six to eight feet long, compared with twenty-four to thirty feet for the trilithon uprights—the missing eight might have been carted away by local farmers for use as building material.

The bluestones have been shaped more precisely than the great sarcens. Was this because they served a special purpose, or because they were made far later in time when better tools existed? In addition, while most of the bluestones are flat on top, two have traces of tenons. Were they once uprights of a bluestone trilithon?

Other Bluestones

More dolomite bluestones are arranged outside the trilithons, but this time in a complete circle about seventy-five feet in diameter. The stones are about the same height as those of the bluestone horseshoe, but are far less regular in shape.

Many look like elongated boulders, which is exactly what they are—all untouched by tools except for two, which appear to have been added later and might have been lintels in the bluestone horseshoe. Why the majority are so much more crude than the horseshoe bluestones is yet another mystery. So is the question of whether the horseshoe bluestones were once trilithons, and, if so, why were they changed?

Many of the stones in the circle are missing, and since they are not spaced at the same distance from one another, it is difficult to tell how many there might have been. Most

Dolomite bluestones found at Stonehenge are not native to the area, raising questions about their origin.

experts estimate somewhere between thirty and forty. Twenty-nine have survived in various degrees. Six are still upright, five are leaning, eight have fallen, and ten are only stumps, either just above the ground or buried just beneath it.

The Sarcen Circle

Finally, about 12 feet outside the bluestone circle, is the sarcen circle, once a mighty ring of uprights and lintels connected to one another. When completed, there were thirty uprights, their inner faces making an almost perfect circle 97 feet across. They are smaller than their inner trilithon cousins, averaging 18 feet in length. They were carefully set in holes from 3 to 5 feet deep so that the tops would be $13\frac{1}{2}$ feet from ground level.

Atop the uprights was a continuous series of thirty lintels, each resting on half of an upright. The lintels were secured to the uprights not only by a mortise-and-tenon system, but also to one another by tongues and grooves, another technique borrowed from carpentry. Vertical grooves were cut into one end of each lintel, into which fit corresponding vertical tongues from their neighbors. Unlike the bluestone circle uprights, the stones of the sarcen circle have been dressed with care, their surfaces bearing the marks of tools.

Seventeen of the thirty uprights are still standing. Eight have fallen, some of them breaking into several pieces, and five are missing entirely. Even more of the lintels— twenty-two—have disappeared. Only $10\frac{1}{2}$ feet long, they probably were the easiest of all the Stonehenge blocks to be dragged away for some other purpose.

Of the remaining lintels, six remain in position atop the uprights, three of them in a row on the northeast facing the open end of the horseshoe. This series of six uprights and three lintels provides a good idea of how impressive the entire unbroken circle must have been.

The complex from the sarcen circle inward to the Altar Stone is the popular public concept of Stonehenge, but there is much more that is often overlooked. Far outside the sarcen circle is another circle, this one of earth, that completely surrounds the stones inside. This circle, which is about 330 feet in diameter, consists of an immense ditch with a raised bank just inside it. The bank and ditch are each about 20 feet wide, and the circle has a gap of about 50 feet opposite the open end of the horseshoe.

Ditch and Bank

The ditch and bank have been greatly filled in and smoothed out over the centuries and are hard to visualize from ground level. The ditch, once perhaps seven feet deep, is now only a shallow depression. The bank, two feet above ground level at the most, was more than six feet high when built. It seems highly likely that the bank was created by earth and chalk taken from the ditch, but the question is whether the builders intended to dig a ditch and got the bank as a by-product or the other way around.

Around the circumference of the bank are three additional stones and two holes where stones once stood. The largest, a twenty-one-foot, roughly dressed sarcen, lies flat just inside the right edge of the gap opposite the horseshoe. Observers in the 1700s, looking at rainwater pooled in the hollows on its upper surface, called it the Slaughter Stone, imagining that these same hollows might have held the blood of sacrificial victims.

The Station Stones are just inside the bank, one at a point almost due west of the main structure and the other on the northwest side. The one on the west is about nine feet long and has fallen, but the other still stands, though only about four feet high.

Also just inside the bank are two small earthen mounds almost exactly due north and south from the stone circle.

Holes have been found in each where other Station Stones once stood. Since lines drawn between the barrows and between the Station Stones cross in the exact center of the main structure, experts think they were used as a measuring device.

The Slaughter Stone lies near the perimeter of Stonehenge's earthen bank. The Heel Stone stands behind.

The Aubrey Holes

Some very important parts of the Stonehenge puzzle are not even visible today. These are three concentric rings of holes between the bank and the sarcen circle. The outermost, just inside the bank, was first noted in the 1600s by antiquarian John Aubrey. Following Aubrey's notes, R.S. Newell rediscovered the holes in the twentieth century and named them for Aubrey.

Fifty-six Aubrey Holes form a 288-foot circle. Originally, they were thirty to seventy inches wide and twenty-four to forty-five inches deep. They do not appear ever to have held either stone uprights or wooden poles. Thirty-four have been excavated and in some were found cremated human bones, but they seem to have been placed there long after the holes were dug. The Aubrey Holes have figured prominently in the intense speculation as to the purpose of Stonehenge.

The other two rings—named the Y and Z holes, since the Aubrey Holes were first called X for unknown—lie inside, much closer to the sarcen circle. The distances are not uniform, but the Z holes are an average of twelve feet from the sarcens and the Y holes thirty-six feet. They are more or less the same shape—an oblong six feet by four feet. The average depth is forty-one inches for the Z holes, thirty-six for the Y holes.

Each ring has thirty holes—the same number as the sarcen uprights—and each Y and Z hole seems to be aligned with a sarcen, like points of invisible spokes on a wheel. The holes seem to have been designed to hold uprights, but no one has been able to find evidence that any stones were placed in them. Part of the mystery is whether the Y and Z holes had some other purpose or were simply part of a project that was abandoned for some reason.

Yet another set of holes, named Q and R by researchers, was dug at one point. They appear to have once held stones, but no one is sure why the stones were subsequently removed.

The Avenue

Not all the mysteries of Stonehenge lie within the circumference of the ditch. Extending far beyond are traces of the Avenue, a forty-foot-wide boulevard with a bank and ditch extending another thirty feet on each side. The Avenue, almost undoubtedly the main processional entrance to Stonehenge, forks east and west a few hundred yards from the monument.

In the center of the Avenue, about seventy-two feet beyond the circular ditch and so close to the highway that one can almost reach over the fence and touch it, is the Heel Stone. This sixteen-foot sarcen boulder in a shallow depression leans sharply toward the monument, although it probably originally stood upright. How the stone got its name is uncertain. Some think it was first used by Aubrey, who wrote about a large stone in a hollow shaped like a human heel. Others, since some older records use a spelling of "hele," think it is from *helios*, the Greek word for "sun." This is particularly important because of the Heel Stone's relationship with the sunrise at midsummer.

Studies have shown that the Heel Stone sits almost directly under the rising sun during the summer solstice.

Post Holes

Also within the Avenue, between the Heel Stone and Slaughter Stone, are two holes where sarcens are thought to have stood, although they probably were smaller than the Heel Stone. Post holes also abound in this same area. More than twenty are clustered between the gap in the ditch, varying in size and in no recognizable pattern, and may only have held scaffolding. More important are the four post holes, A1 through A4, just outside the Heel Stone depression to the north. They are evenly spaced and lie in a straight line at a right angle to the Avenue. No evidence of stone or post remains in them, but they must have been used for something. The question is, for what?

This, indeed, is the question that lingers after a survey of all that remains of Stonehenge—this tumbledown collection of ditches, banks, standing stones, fallen stones, and mysterious holes. We know what its physical shape now is. Over the centuries, investigators have pieced together how it must have originally appeared. But even as their knowledge increased regarding what Stonehenge was, the central mystery—what it was for—only grew more complex.

Chapter 2

Merlin and Magic

O ften, when facts are in short supply, people must rely
on fancy, and few objects on earth have yielded themselves more to the fanciful than Stonehenge. Conjecture has
followed conjecture over the centuries, many based on little
more than vivid imagination, and neither time nor knowledge has been able to stop them. One writer more than two
hundred years ago observed that "the mazes of wild opinion
are more complex and intricate than the ruin."[3]

Such mazes had their beginning in the Middle Ages. It
was a time when it was natural to believe in the supernatural.
Virtually everyone accepted the existence of witchcraft and
magic. If God was real and immediate to the people of the
time, so was Satan and his legion of devils and evil spirits
on which all sorts of mysterious happenings could be
blamed. It was inevitable, therefore, that the earliest explanations of Stonehenge were rooted in magic.

It was easier to dismiss the other large stone monuments in Britain. Their uprights, even though carefully laid
out, were rough and unfinished and could be explained as
something "in which by a whim of the Creator the stones
stood on end and in some sort of order."[4] Stonehenge was
different. Most of the blocks had obviously been shaped,
and some bore tool marks.

An eighteenth-century painting portrays Stonehenge as a mystical monument beneath an ominous sky.

And yet, it was difficult for the people of the Middle Ages to believe that Stonehenge was man-made. As late as the 1560s, a bishop of Salisbury said he thought it was beyond the combined efforts of everyone in his area to move a single stone. And so, in the medieval mind, if Stonehenge was not naturally formed and not made by humans, it must have been made by magic.

Geoffrey of Monmouth

Only a few years after Henry of Huntingdon wrote that none could say how Stonehenge was built, another writer set out to do so. About 1136 Geoffrey of Monmouth wrote his *History of the Kings of Britain*. Geoffrey was never much troubled by an absence of facts, freely blending truth, legend, and invention. Although a modern expert, Stuart Piggott, called him "the least reliable and most suspect chronicler of the Middle Ages,"[5] Geoffrey's book had an enormous influence on how future history, including that of Stonehenge, was written.

Medicinal Properties

The stones of Stonehenge were long thought to have the power to heal. Even in modern times, people have brought sick relatives to lie on the stones, hoping that some miraculous power would bring a cure. The legend can be traced to Geoffrey of Monmouth who wrote about Stonehenge in the early 1100s.

According to Geoffrey, Merlin the magician told the British king Aurelius that the stones for a new monument should come from Ireland. Aurelius laughed, whereupon Merlin said, in this version quoted in *The Making of Stonehenge* by Rodney Castledean:

> Try not to give way to foolish laughter, your majesty. . . . There is nothing absurd in what I am suggesting. These stones contain a mystery and a healing virtue against many ailments. Giants of old carried them from the furthest ends of Africa and set them up in Ireland at the time when they lived there. Whenever they felt ill, it was their custom to prepare baths at the foot of the stones; they used to pour water over the stones into baths in which the sick were cured. They also used to mix the water with herbal concoctions to heal their wounds. There is not a single stone among them which has not some medicinal property.

According to Geoffrey, Stonehenge was a monument set up about 485 to commemorate a great victory of the British king Aurelius Ambrosius, who may or may not have ever existed, over Saxon invaders. Aurelius calls on the great magician, Merlin, who advises him to import the Giants' Ring from Ireland. In Merlin's description, the Giants' Ring is made of stones so large that "there is no one alive strong enough to move them. If they are placed in a position round this site, in the way they are put up over there, they will stand for ever."[6]

Merlin goes on to say that the stones had been taken to Ireland from Africa by giants and that they have magic powers. Supposedly, a person who bathes in water that has been used to wash the stones will be cured of all disease.

Ambrosius sends his brother, Uther Pendragon, and an army of fifteen thousand men to Ireland where they defeat local troops and proceed to the area of present-day Kildare. They reach the Giants' Ring but are unable to shift the

Merlin broods before an upright stone. Medieval legend held that the magician was responsible for erecting Stonehenge.

huge stones. Merlin appears, laughs, and plucks the stones from the ground. After they are carried to the plain in southern Britain where the British dead from the battle have been buried, Merlin "puts up the stones round the British sepulcher [tomb] in just the same way as they had stood in Ireland."[7] Eventually, Geoffrey writes, Ambrosius is buried within Stonehenge.

Geoffrey's Critics

Not everyone accepted the accuracy of Geoffrey's book. He claimed to have gotten his facts from some ancient volume, but no one at the time knew of such a book. As one of his contemporaries, William of Newburgh, pointed out, highly reliable chroniclers such as the Venerable Bede in the 500s made no mention of Arthur or Stonehenge. William went so far as to write that "everything this man [Geoffrey] wrote" might have stemmed from "an inordinate love of lying."[8]

Lies or not, Geoffrey's tales about ancient England took firm root. Merlin's name was to be linked with Stonehenge for another six hundred years. Robert Wace used Geoffrey's story in his French history of England, written in 1155. Wace's version, in turn, was picked up and passed on by a priest named Layamon about 1200. A manuscript from the 1300s shows Merlin, about twice the height of an ordinary man, placing a lintel on an upright. An illustrated history of the world from the same period depicts a curiously square version of Stonehenge, which it says was built in the year 483 by "the enchanter Merlin, solely by virtue of his art and not force."[9]

The story was passed along for centuries in various forms and was given its largest circulation in 1482 when William Caxton printed a version, one of the first in English. In it, once the stones are in place, Ambrosius "thanked Merlyn and richely him rewarded at his own wylle & that place lete calle Stonhenge for evermore."[10]

Polydore Vergil

Geoffrey's story began to lose momentum when challenged by such prominent historians as Polydore Vergil. Commissioned by King Henry VII in 1505 to write a history of England, Vergil rejected most of Geoffrey's version, accusing him of "enhauncinge them [the ancient British] with moste impudent lyeing."[11]

Such a popular story, however, is hard to kill, and Geoffrey's stayed alive. John Leland, writing thirty years after Vergil, names Merlin as the builder of Stonehenge, although he denies the stones were brought from Ireland. And Edmund Spenser's epic romance *The Faerie Queene*, dedicated and given to Queen Elizabeth I in 1590, has Ambrosius buried at Stonehenge, although Merlin is not mentioned as its builder.

Monument to Treason

According to the twelfth-century chronicler Geoffrey of Monmouth, Stonehenge was built as a monument to ancient British nobles who were treacherously murdered while supposedly the guests of the Saxon king Hengist. The Briton Vortigern unseats the rightful king Aurelius with the help of his (Vortigern's) son and Hengist, whose daughter is Vortigern's wife. Hengist invites Vortigern to a supposedly peaceful meeting, but during the meeting gives a sign to his followers, who pull their daggers and murder the British.

Edmund Spenser, in his 1590 epic *The Faerie Queene*, describes, as quoted in *Stonehenge Complete* by Christopher Chippindale, how:

But by the help of Virtimere his
    sonne,
He [Vortigern] is again unto his rule
    restored, And Hengist seeming
    sad, for that was donne,
Received is to grace and new accord,
Through his faire daughters face, and
    flattring word;
Soone after which, three hundred
    Lordes he slew
Of British bl…, all sitting at his
    bord;
Whose dolefull monuments who list
    to rew,
Th'eternall markes of treason may at
    Stoneheng vew.

One reason for the enduring popularity of and belief in the Merlin story was its great appeal to English kings and nobility. England was just beginning to assume a leading role in European affairs in the 1400s and 1500s after taking a backseat to France. It was little wonder that, at a time when they sought glory on the battlefield by day, the nobility of England would relax at night listening to tales of the long-ago glory of their ancestors.

Folklore

Stonehenge came to be associated with magic and Merlin not only in scholarly chronicles, but also in folklore. According to one popular story, first printed in 1660 but probably much older, Merlin asks Satan for help in moving the stones from Ireland to Salisbury Plain. So, disguised as a gentleman, Satan approaches an old woman guarding the stones. Pouring a quantity of strangely numbered coins in front of her, he tells her she may have as much as she can add up while the stones are being loaded for departure.

The old woman agrees, thinking that it will take a long time, if ever, to move such huge stones. No sooner has she placed her finger on the first coin, however, when Satan shouts that the stones are ready. She looks up to see the stones bound together like a bundle of sticks. Satan lifts the stones on his shoulder and flies off, leaving the old woman with her single coin.

According to the story, on the flight to Salisbury Plain, one stone slips out of the bundle and falls in the Avon River. Indeed, such a stone can still be seen in the river near Bulford eleven miles east of Stonehenge, but investigation showed it to be far smaller than the other stones, and it had a modern iron ring embedded in one end.

Stonehenge on Stage

Eventually, superstition gave way to reason, and the Merlin-Stonehenge saga was put down to legend rather than put forward as fact. By now, however, it had taken a firm grip on the imagination of the public, who were not ready to give it up. It disappeared from historical accounts, only to reappear in a new role—a stage role, in fact.

Plays featuring Merlin enjoyed a run of popularity in the early 1600s, but most of their scripts have disappeared. One that has survived is that of *The Birth of Merlin*, once thought to be a lost work of William Shakespeare but actually written by Thomas Rowley.

In the play Merlin is depicted, as he frequently was in literature, as the son of Satan and an unwilling earthly woman, named Joan Go-to-'t in this telling. In the final act, Satan reappears, accompanied by a horde of evil spirits, intending to force himself on Joan. The young Merlin pops up, banishes the spirits, and entraps Satan in a large rock. Having saved his mother, Merlin tells her:

Merlin was a central figure in the folklore surrounding Stonehenge for many centuries.

And when you die I will erect a monument
Upon the verdant plains of Salisbury
No king shall have so high a sepulcher,
With pendulous stones that I will hang by art,
Where neither lime nor mortar shall be used,
A dark enigma to thy memory.[12]

Merlin's supposed association with Stonehenge was the theme of several seventeenth- and eighteenth-century plays.

Plays about Merlin vanished, along with virtually all other forms of drama, during the strict Puritan rule over England in the mid-1600s, when many forms of public amusement were banned. They reappeared afterward, and as late as 1734 a musical pantomime, *Merlin; or, the Devil of Stone-Henge* by John Galliard, was performed in London. Pantomime had a different meaning in those days. Dialogue was used, but it was sung instead of spoken. The show usually was short, used as an encore to the main performance, and depended chiefly on visual effects.

The Devil of Stone-Henge weaves several legendary figures into its plot. Merlin shares the stage with Dr. Faustus, who in German folklore is supposed to have sold his soul to Satan in exchange for youth and riches. Stonehenge appears in two scenes. In the first, the ghost of Dr. Faustus wanders among the stones before Merlin appears and banishes him to Hades. In the second, "a pleasant Prospect of the Infernal Regions," the plain is filled with young female "Nymphs of these Plains, all courteous and free"[13] who dance around the stone circle.

A Short Run

Even though the dancing nymphs included Susannah Cibber, widely popular as one of the most beautiful actresses in England, *The Devil of Stone-Henge* lasted only five performances. New ideas about who built Stonehenge and why were on the horizon—ideas grounded in logic instead of a reliance on magic.

Some people defiantly clung to Geoffrey's account as historical fact. John Lewis, in his 1724 *History of Great Britain*, dismisses criticism of the story by others, mainly Polydore Vergil, as "false surmise to cover his own Ignorance."[14] By 1860, however, historian John Thurman was dismissing the Merlin story as "a bare-faced invention, and full of old wives' tales, and idle stories."[15]

Stonehenge's association with the supernatural and legendary, however, has never entirely vanished. Even Polydore Vergil, Geoffrey's most persistent critic, thought the monument was the tomb of legendary Aurelius Ambrosius. In our own day, articles appear suggesting that Stonehenge was built by giants or even by outer space aliens.

Samuel Daniel, writing in 1599, lamented the lack of facts and records on Stonehenge and how its very antiquity had forced people to invent stories of magic to explain what was likely one of the wonders of human ingenuity. He wrote:

> The Ignorance, with fabulous discourse,
> Robbing faire Arte and Cunning of their right,
> Tels, how those stones, were by the Devil's force,

From *Affrike* brought to *Ireland* at night,
And thense, to Britannie, by *Magicke* course,
From Gyants hands redeem'd by Merlin's sleight. . .
With this old Legend then Credulite [belief]
Holdes her content, and closes up her care.[16]

Man, Not "Magicke"

By the 1600s, most educated persons had come to the conclusion that Stonehenge had probably been built by man, not
"magicke." William Lambarde wrote that there was nothing
all that supernatural about Stonehenge and that the stones
had been erected "with no more Wonder than one Post of a
House hangeth above another, seinge that all the Stones are
lett one in another by a Mortece and Tenant [tenon], as
Carpenters call them." In addition, he saw the moving of the
stones as no great feat, providing there were enough muscles
and enough money, writing that "by Art [skill], Thinges of
greater Weight may be removed, especially if a Prince be
Pay-maister."[17]

The time had also come when curious people would not
be willing, as Sir John Harrington, godson of Queen
Elizabeth I, suggested, to "rather marvel at [the stones] than
tell either why or how they were set there."[18] The
Renaissance, a rebirth of classical learning in Europe, had
ushered in a new spirit in inquiry. Stonehenge was now to be
studied rather than marveled at. If it had indeed been built by
men, who were they?

Chapter 3

Romans, Danes, and Phoenicians

In the 1600s educated persons in England began looking at Stonehenge in a new way. They were no longer content to argue among themselves on the merits of ancient stories. Instead, they were filled with a spirit of inquiry. William Stukeley, who was to play a major role in the investigation wrote, "After the Reformation, upon the Revival of Learning among us, the Curious began to consider it [Stonehenge] more intimately."[19]

Instead of examining centuries-old texts for clues, serious investigators began to study the structure itself, comparing it with others around the world. Acknowledging that it had been built by men instead of through magic, they examined Britain's past. Who, among the many peoples who had come to the island, whether as settlers or conquerors, had been capable of such a feat? They examined and argued over almost every possible answer, but they would dismiss—strangely enough—the most obvious one.

One of the events that accelerated investigation of Stonehenge was a royal command. Stonehenge had begun to become a tourist attraction and in 1620 received its most distinguished visitor. King James I stopped by on his way to see George Villers, duke of Buckingham, who was living at Wilton, about ten miles south of Stonehenge.

The king was fascinated by what he saw and told Buckingham so. Perhaps intending to make a gift of Stonehenge to his royal master, the duke offered to buy it from Robert Newdyk, owner of the surrounding land, but Newdyk declined the offer.

To satisfy James's curiosity, however, Buckingham—presumably with Newdyk's permission—had a hole dug in the middle of the stone circle. John Aubrey, writing more than forty years later, reported that in the still visible excavation had been found animal horns and antlers, arrowheads, rusted armor, and bones—whether human or animal he could not say. Something else was apparently found, but Aubrey wrote that "what it was Mrs Mary Trotman [from a nearby farm] hath forgot."[20]

Inigo Jones

King James's curiosity was not satisfied. He decided that a complete study of Stonehenge should be undertaken and appointed his royal surveyor of works, Inigo Jones, to do the job. Jones was considered the finest architect in England, having studied in Italy under the great Italian master Palladio in the styles of ancient Greece and Rome. His training led him to believe that all great works came from such classical traditions, and it was this viewpoint that colored his opinions on Stonehenge.

Jones worked at Stonehenge on and off from 1633 to 1640, but on his death in 1652 left only "some few indigested notes"[21] to be assembled and added to by his colleague and son-in-law, John Webb. The result, in 1655, was the first full-length book on Stonehenge—*The Most Notable Antiquity of Great Britain, Vulgarly Called Stone-heng, on Salisbury Plain. Restored by Inigo Jones, Esquire.*

After studying Stonehenge for nearly a decade, architect Inigo Jones concluded that it was the work of Roman invaders.

Jones or Webb—no one can be sure which man wrote which parts of the book—praises Stonehenge as being both beautiful and elegant. Thus, they say, it could not have been built, as according to Geoffrey's story, by the ancient Britons, whom they dismiss as "a savage and barbarous People, knowing no use at all of garments . . . much less any knowledge had they to erect stately structures, or such remarkable Works as Stoneheng."[22]

No, Jones and Webb wrote, people must look elsewhere to find the builders of Stonehenge, to "even such a flourishing Age, as when *Architecture* in rare Perfection, and such *People* lookt upon, as by continual Success, attaining unto the sole Power over *Arts,* as well as *Empires,* commanded all."[23] In other words, Stonehenge was so grand that it could have been built only by the Romans.

Roman Invaders

The theory that Romans built Stonehenge was not as far-fetched as it might seem. Roman legions under the emperor Claudius had invaded Britain in A.D. 54 and secured most of the island as a Roman colony. They would remain in power for about four hundred years, pushing the Britons north into Scotland and west into Wales and Cornwall. During their centuries of occupation, the Romans built villas, theaters, and temples in the classical style.

As evidence for their theory, Jones and Webb pointed out the classical proportions of Stonehenge—six trilithons laid out in a perfect hexagon, their planes forming four equilateral triangles within the stone circle. The problem is that Stonehenge contains five trilithons, not six, and even if there had in the distant past been a sixth, the remaining five do not fit in a hexagonal shape.

Geometry aside, however, it is hard to understand why—apart from their absolute devotion to classical architecture—Jones and Webb would have considered Stonehenge Roman. The many Roman ruins in Britain resembled their counterparts in Italy—graceful columns, tile mosaics, and carved ornamentation. Stonehenge has none of these. Why would the Romans have built something so crude?

The book was roundly criticized when it was published. Very few copies were sold, and most of those printed were still in storage at the publisher when they were destroyed by the Great Fire of London in 1666. A contemporary historian, Edmund Bolton, wrote that the Romans "were wont to make stones vocall by inscriptions. That STONAGE was a worke of the Britanns, the rudeness it selfe perswades."[24] His own theory was that Stonehenge was a memorial to British queen Boadicea, who led a revolt against the Romans in A.D. 70.

Chipping Away

Antiquarians were not the only people to become interested in Stonehenge during the 1600s. It was in this century that the structure began to draw visitors, to become a tourist attraction. As is too often the case with ancient monuments, many of the visitors wanted to take away a piece of Stonehenge as a souvenir.

In 1654 John Evelyn, visiting his uncle's nearby farm, stopped by Stonehenge and found "the stone so exceedingly hard, that all my strength with a hammer could not break a fragment." And Dr. William Stukeley complained in 1740 about the "detestable practice" and "unaccountable folly" of "breaking pieces off with great hammers" by people who thought the stones able to cure diseases.

Some people excused themselves in the name of science. A Mrs. Powys, although she thought it as "an absurd curiosity for people to wish the remains of the temple further ruined," nevertheless wrote to a friend that "I was Obliged with a Hammer to labour hard three Quarters of an Hour to get but one Ounce and a half" for an experiment.

Shortly before 1900 someone asked Sir Edmund Antrobus, owner of Stonehenge, what should be done if a visitor was seen hammering away. Sir Edmund's advice was to "offer one of those good-natured remonstrances which will carry weight with the offender, and are sure to enlist the sympathy and assistance of the great body of bystanders."

Despite the vigilance of caretakers, tourists continued to try to chip off pieces with hammers smuggled in under their coats. Finally, because both the danger of vandalism and the crush of tourists became so great (more than 1 million visitors a year), Stonehenge's guardian, the English Heritage organization, closed off access to the stones themselves. Visitors now must stay on a path taking them across the bank and ditch to within about twenty feet of the westernmost sarcen.

Another critic of the book, an antiquarian named Dr. Glisson, thought Stonehenge was much older—"at least three or four thousand years old longe before ye Romans."[25] The good doctor gave no reasons as to how he came up with such a figure, but it would turn out to be astonishingly accurate.

The Roman theory was much like Geoffrey's story in that, although widely discredited, it endured. As recently as the mid-1960s, privately published pamphlets claimed Roman origins for the monument.

The Danes

Many of the critics who rejected the Roman theory nevertheless agreed with Jones and Webb that the ancient
Britons lacked the ability to have built Stonehenge. They
continued to look to distant lands for origins. For instance,
if the Romans had not built Stonehenge during their occupation of Britain, perhaps the Danes had.

The Danes—the name given to Viking invaders
although some were from Norway—had begun ravaging
the British coast in the early 700s and settled in northeast
England in large numbers. They were eventually defeated
by the Saxon king Alfred the Great and were absorbed into
the population.

In 1663, Dr. Walter Charleton, royal physician to King
Charles II, suggested that Danish settlers had built
Stonehenge. He based his theory on correspondence with a
Danish investigator, Olaus Worm, who had written to him
about "*dysser*", large stone tombs in Denmark.

The Danish theory fared no better than the Roman
one. Numerous chronicles had survived from the 800s, and
none mentioned the Danes building any monuments.
Furthermore, as many writers pointed out, the Danish
dysser were not stone circles like Stonehenge but were
much more like dolmen tombs.

A Bow to Royalty

That failed to deter Dr. Charleton, who proposed that
Stonehenge's circle resembled a crown and therefore was
probably a site where Danish kings were crowned. This
was a theory sure to find favor with the doctor's patron,
Charles II, who had visited Stonehenge while hiding out
from a Puritan army during the English Revolution in
1651. Charles had been restored to his throne in 1660,
only three years prior to the publication of Dr. Charleton's
book, and the author took pains to link the king with his

Dyssers *(large stone tombs) found in Denmark led to the theory that the Danes built Stonehenge.*

theory. The dedication includes a poem by John Dryden with the following verse:

> These Ruins sheltred once *His* Sacred Head,
> Then when from *Wor'ster's* fatal Field *He* fled;
> Watch'd by the Genius of this Kingly Place,
> And mighty Visions of the Danish Race.
> His *Refuge* then was for a *Temple* shown:
> But, *He* Restor'd, 'tis now become a *Throne.*[26]

Just as Jones and Webb had interpreted Stonehenge in terms of their own vision of what architecture should be, Dr. Charleton's theory was colored by the popularity of all things connected with the monarchy after its restoration. Webb, in fact, included a long and flowery dedication to Charles II in his book, refuting Charleton's view and defending those of himself and Jones.

Anglo-Saxons

Other foreign settlers of Britain who might have built Stonehenge were the Anglo-Saxons, who invaded the island soon after the departure of the Romans. Indeed, a German scholar suggested this in 1720, but the stone monuments in Germany—like those in Denmark—were completely unlike Stonehenge. Also, surviving Anglo-Saxon chronicles mention nothing about building anything remotely similar.

With the most likely non-Briton builders eliminated, speculation turned further afield. Antiquarian Aylett Sammes attempted to link ancient British culture with that of the eastern Mediterranean. In a 1676 book he dismissed Geoffrey of Monmouth's story, but proposed a solution even more imaginative. He wrote, "Why may not these Giants, so often mentioned, upon this, and other occasions, be the Phoenicians, as we have proved on other occasions, and the Art of erecting these Stones, instead of the STONES themselves, brought from the farthermost parts of *Africa*, the known habitations of the Phoenicians."[27]

Phoenicians

According to Sammes, the Phoenicians, led by Hercules, sailed around Spain to discover Britain. He pointed out that Inigo Jones had compared Stonehenge to temples in Greece and Italy, both of which Sammes said sprang from the Phoenicians. Sammes offered little else in the way of proof of a Phoenician connection with Stonehenge, but his speculation led the way for others in subsequent centuries who might say, in the absence of any absolute proof to the contrary, that their ideas might be correct.

At least, as speculations about the builders flew back and forth, some progress was made about the origins of the building itself. John Rastell, writing about the same time as Polydore Vergil, claimed that the large sarcens were so unlike any other building stone that they must be artificial. Since they were too large to have been quarried, he said, they must have been "artificially cemented into that hard and durable Substance from some large Congeries of Sand, and other unctuous matter mixed together."[28]

Source of the Sarcens

The sarcen stones, once believed to be of Irish origin, were actually transported twenty miles to Stonehenge from Marlborough Downs.

The truth was much simpler and closer at hand. As far back as 1580 William Lambarde, in rejecting Geoffrey's story that the stones came from Ireland, said, "There is within the same Shyre great Stoare of Stone of the same Kinde, namely, above Marlborow."[29] Sir John Harrington agreed and claimed that the old name for Marlborough was Merlinsburie, still clinging to the Merlin story.

Indeed, sarcen boulders still can be seen on the Marlborough Downs about twenty miles north of Stonehenge and a few miles east of Avebury. Few are as large as those in Stonehenge, and archaeologists have speculated that most of the larger stones have been broken up over the centuries for use as building material.

If Marlborough Downs is the source for the sarcens—and no one has found a closer site or a more logical explanation—the builders of Stonehenge could have used two routes to transport them south. After being floated across the Kennet River on huge barges, the stones could have been dragged overland on sledges. These wooden platforms, under which were probably placed a series of rolling logs, would have been dragged by ropes west and then south, avoiding the branches of the Avon River.

The other route might have been due south to the Avon, where the stones would have been loaded onto barges and floated the remaining distance. This route is much more direct, and floating the stones would have been far easier than dragging them. The problem is that to get to the river, the builders would have had to drag the heavy stones and sledges across miles of marshland.

A British Monument

By the 1700s most scholars had rejected the notion that Stonehenge had been built by foreign invaders, and traveler Samuel Gale could write in confidence, "I conclude it to be a British monument, the Romans always leaving indisputable marks of their grandeur . . . of any of which our Stone-henge has not the least resemblance."[30]

And yet, if some parts of the mystery of Stonehenge were more clear, others remained hidden. The sarcens might have come from Marlborough Downs, but what about the bluestones? Nothing like them existed in

England. And if Britons had indeed been the builders, how long ago had they labored and why?

Up to the 1700s, the study of Stonehenge had relied mainly on the searching of ancient documents, comparing the monument with those in other lands, and mere guesswork. So-called experts wrote volumes defending their own theories and attacking those of others. Few of them had paid much attention to the structure itself, but this was about to change. New generations of investigators would begin a painstaking study of Stonehenge in the continuing effort to unravel its mysteries.

Chapter 4

Aubrey, Stukeley, and the Druids

After centuries of looking first to magic, then to distant lands for the builders of Stonehenge, investigators concluded it was a product of the ancient Britons. They then began to study it in terms of the structure itself and its relation to the hundreds of other such monuments in Britain. Although their methods were sound, they followed a false trail to a conclusion that would obscure the truth about Stonehenge for generations.

The trail began with the work of John Aubrey, who was familiar with Stonehenge since his boyhood, having been born in the nearby village of Easton Pierse in 1626. A lawyer by training, he had a wide variety of interests. He wrote a best-selling collection of biographies titled *Brief Lives* and was enough of a scientist to be named a Fellow of the Royal Society, an academy of scientists. He also had one of the largest collections of natural curiosities in the country and wrote books on folklore and place names.

Aubrey's great passions, however, were the ancient monuments that dotted his native Wiltshire. "I was inclin'd by my

Genius, from my Childhood to the Love of Antiquities," as he later wrote, "and my Fate dropt me in a Country most suitable for such Enquiries . . . Salisbury-Plaines, and Stonehenge I had known from eight years old."[31]

Aubrey's study was done by royal command. In 1663 King Charles II was discussing Stonehenge with Dr. Charleton when the subject of Avebury came up. Charleton told the king that Aubrey had said that Avebury outshined Stonehenge "as a Cathedral does a Parish Church."[32] Intrigued, the king sent for Aubrey, who displayed a drawing of Avebury. Charles was so impressed that two weeks later he had Aubrey take him on a tour.

John Aubrey studied the ancient monuments at Avebury and Stonehenge and believed that both were the work of Druids.

Aubrey's Assignment

As a result of the visit, the king ordered Aubrey to write him a "description" of Avebury. The king's brother, the future James II, added that Aubrey should include an "account of the Old Camps and Barrows on the Plaines,"[33] including Stonehenge. Aubrey's habit was to let small projects turn into huge ones that somehow were never finished. His description evolved into a gigantic manuscript titled *Monumenta Britannica*, which was never completed or published in printed form, but nevertheless was to have a great impact on the world's view of Stonehenge.

Aubrey sought knowledge of Stonehenge not in books but in the work itself. Stonehenge and other sites, he wrote, were "so exceeding old that no Bookes doe reach them, so that there is no way to retrive them but by comparative antiqutie, which I have writt upon the spott, from the Monuments themselves."[34] He studied hundreds of sites, took endless measurements, and made copious notes. He discovered at Stonehenge what he called "cavities" inside the bank, which centuries later were named the Aubrey Holes in his honor.

His studies led him to believe that Stonehenge and most of the other stone circles in the British Isles were temples of some sort. No other explanation made any sense. However, Aubrey then jumped to the conclusion that would long dominate the public's view of Stonehenge. "My presumption is," he wrote, "that the Druids being the most eminent Priests, or Order of Priests, among the Britaines; 'tis odds [likely], but that these ancient monuments were Temples of the Priests of the most eminent Order, viz. [that is] Druids."[35]

The Phoenician Influence

English antiquarian Aylett Sammes agreed with John Aubrey that Stonehenge was a Druid temple, but whereas Aubrey believed the Druids to be native to Britain, Sammes thought they had come from Greece in Phoenician ships. In this quotation from his 1676 book *Britannia Antiqua Illustrata,* which is found in *Stonehenge Complete* by Christopher Chippindale, he describes the Druids thusly:

The next Order of People in Britain were the Druids, who did not totally abolish all the Customs and Opinions of the Bards [the former British priests], but retained the most useful parts of them, such as the Immortality of the Soul, to which they added the Transmigration of it, according to the opinion of Pythagoras [a Greek philosopher and mathematician], about whose time, or a little after, I believe the Greeks entered this island. Moreover they continued the customes of rehearsing things in Verse, which they either brought out of Greece, or continued it as they found it established here.

In this artist's rendition, Druids gather around Stonehenge's sarcen circle during a religious ceremony.

The Druids

The Druids had, indeed, been the priests of the inhabitants of Britain before the coming of the Romans, but very little was known about them. The Roman general Julius Caesar, writing about his campaigns in Gaul (modern France), reported that human sacrifice was part of the Druidical religion. A Roman historian, Diodorus Siculus, said further that the Druids "kill a man by knife-stab in the region above the midriff, and after his fall they foretell the future by the convulsions of his limbs, and the pouring of his blood."[36]

Pliny the Elder, a Roman scholar writing some time later, described the Druids as less bloodthirsty. They were said to conduct worship around sacred oak trees, particularly those on which mistletoe grows. According to Pliny, the Druids practiced sacrifice of animals, not humans. Still later accounts suggest that the Druids abandoned blood sacrifices altogether. They cast spells, made prophecies, and acted as judges.

There was absolutely no evidence to link the Druids with Stonehenge, but that did not stop Aubrey. Indeed, in his later years his theories grew more bizarre. He claimed that since Druids were supposed to be able to talk with eagles, they might have also made gaps between the lintels and uprights of Stonehenge for starlings and could converse with them.

Aubrey's connection between Druids and Stonehenge might have vanished had it not been for Roger Gale and John Toland. Toland, an Irish philosopher, absorbed Aubrey's theories and linked them with stone circles in his country. Gale, who shared Aubrey's interest in ancient monuments, translated *Templa Druidium,* the first part of Aubrey's manuscript, from Latin into English. Both Gale and Toland would become friends of a young Lincolnshire physician, Dr. William Stukeley, one of the most influential men in the history of Stonehenge.

Dr. Stukeley

Like Aubrey, Stukeley was fascinated from his youth onward with ancient monuments. He traveled extensively, was a Fellow of the Royal Society, and was a founder of the Society of Antiquaries in 1718. He had far wider interests, as well, becoming a physician in 1720 and an ordained minister in the Church of England in 1729.

Stukeley's attachment to Stonehenge came even before he saw it. Entranced by a drawing of the monument, he ambitiously set out to make a model of Stonehenge that would include "the original Architectonic Scheme by which it was erected, together with its design, use, Founders, etc."[37] He finally visited the site itself on May 18, 1719, with Roger Gale and Gale's brother, Samuel, and was so captivated that he would spend the summers of 1721 through 1724 working there and at Avebury.

Stukeley was just as thorough in his examination of Stonehenge as Aubrey had been. Indeed, although he did not record Aubrey's "cavities," he made several important discoveries that had escaped the attention of all previous investigators. He was the first to record the Avenue, the parallel banks and ditches extending to the northeast past the Heel Stone, and noted that it had almost been obliterated by cart tracks. In following the Avenue, Stukeley found that it divided a few hundred yards from the monument. He was unable to trace the eastward branch, almost entirely obscured by later development. Its path has subsequently been traced to the bank of the Avon River just beyond the village of Amesbury about two miles east.

Following the western branch of the Avenue, Stukeley discovered a raised area about 2 miles long and 350 feet wide that had been made by digging parallel ditches and piling earth between them. It looked like a racecourse to Stukeley, and he accordingly named it the "cursus." He thought it had been a place where the "British charioteer may have a good opportunity of showing that dexterity spoken of by [Julius] Caesar."[38]

Atop the Lintel

Within Stonehenge itself, Stukeley and those he persuaded to work alongside him took more than two thousand measurements. He even climbed atop a trilithon to measure a lintel. It was five by fifteen feet—large enough, Stukeley later wrote, "for a steady head and nimble feet to dance a minuet on."[39]

Part of Stukeley's mania for measurement was to disprove the lingering notion that Stonehenge had been built by the Romans. Had that been so, he argued, his measurements would be in multiples of Roman feet—about 12 inches. Instead, he proclaimed, the monument had been

planned using the more ancient measure of the cubit—the length of a person's elbow to the tip of the middle finger—which he reckoned at 20.8 inches. And, while he agreed that some of the spacing of the uprights matched that of classical architecture, he said this could be ascribed to an authority older than the Romans—"from pure natural reason and good sense."[40]

In addition to measurements, Stukeley undertook excavations and in so doing discovered how the uprights had been put in place. He found that the builders had dug holes in the solid chalk that lies about a foot under the surface. The uprights were placed in these holes, and flint wedges were hammered into the gaps on each side to hold them firm.

Through meticulous measurements of uprights, lintels, and trilithons, Dr. William Stukeley proved that the Romans did not build Stonehenge.

The Barrows

Not all the excavation was within Stonehenge. Curious if a connection existed between the monument and the nearby barrows, Stukeley began exploring them in 1722. In some he found skeletons, their heads lying in the direction of Stonehenge. In one, along with the skeleton, he found "bits of . . . chippings of the stones of the temple"[41] and concluded that one of the builders had been buried there. This, if true, would further indicate that Stonehenge had been built before the Romans, since Roman roads and other construction had been built on top of similar barrows elsewhere in Britain.

One of Stukeley's observations would, much later, lead to a major branch of Stonehenge research. In the course of his several summers, he found that if one stands at the foot of the central trilithon and looks toward the Heel Stone, the line of sight points to the spot on the horizon "whereabouts the Sun rises, when the days are longest."[42] Indeed, at dawn on the summer solstice (June 21), the longest day of the year, the sun rises almost exactly over the Heel Stone.

Stukeley's discovery would seem to indicate that Stonehenge was some sort of observatory, but he appears to have dismissed this theory. Instead, he concentrated on the fact that, as at other ancient British monuments, the major alignments were a few degrees off from the main points of the compass. He thought that the builders had used a magnetic compass and intended to align the stones accordingly, but that a slight variation in the earth's magnetic field had caused the error.

Such variations do occur, and Stukeley was able to research them, calculating that a variation that would have caused Stonehenge's "misalignment" would last have occurred in 1620 and at prior seven-hundred-year intervals. If Stukeley was correct, then Stonehenge would have been built in A.D. 920, A.D. 220, 460 B.C., and so on. Stukeley chose 460 B.C. as the most likely date.

The Druidical Obsession

Stukeley chose that date not so much as a result of his research as of his increasing obsession with Druidism. As early as 1722 he took the name Chyndonax the Druid as a member of the Society of Roman Knights, a group dedicated to preserving ancient sites. In 1726 he built a Druid "temple" next to a mistletoe-laden apple tree in his garden.

In addition to reading Aubrey's book, he had studied the works of others, particularly Aylett Sammes, the man who proposed the Phoenicians as the builders of Stonehenge. Sammes had contended that the Druids were not native to Europe, but had been carried there in Phoenician ships. Stukeley took Sammes's view further, claiming that the Druids were the direct spiritual descendants of Abraham, Moses, and the other patriarchs of the Bible. His date of 460 B.C. for Stonehenge fit perfectly. It was before the birth of Jesus of Nazareth, which would explain why the Druids were not yet Christians, and it was at a time when Phoenician sea trade had supposedly been at a peak.

Stukeley saw no conflict between his admiration for Druidism and his status as an ordained minister. Indeed, he saw one as a direct descendant of the other. Here was yet another case in which a person's beliefs about Stonehenge were a result of what he wanted to believe, which was that the monument was a testament to the values that Stukeley thought were later embodied in Christianity in general and the Church of England in particular. Stukeley considered the Church of England the true heir of the Druids and the Old Testament Hebrews and, seeing it threatened on one side by Roman

White-robed Druids appear eerily incandescent during a summer solstice ceremony at Stonehenge, much like Stukeley had imagined.

Catholicism and on the other by reformers such as John Wesley, founder of Methodism, wished to underscore its heritage. In the preface to his 1740 book on Stonehenge, subtitled *A Temple Restor'd to the British Druids*, he wrote that his purpose was

> besides preserving the memory of these extraordinary monuments . . . to promote . . . the knowledge and practice of ancient and true Religion; to revive . . . that true sense of Religion which keeps the medium between ignorant superstition and learned free-thinking, between enthusiasm and the rational worship of God, which is no where upon earth done, in my judgement better than in the Church of England.[43]

Facts and Fantasy

As a result, Stukeley's books on Stonehenge and the one on Avebury published in 1743 mixed his excellent archaeological research with what modern writer Christopher Chippindale calls "fantastical Druidic vapourings."[44] Stukeley calls forth visions of white-robed Druids processing up the Avenue to sacrifice animals inside the sarcen circle. British nobles stand close by, while ordinary people watch from the circular bank outside. His basic unit of measurement is called the Druid's cubit, and Thomas Hayward, on whose land Stonehenge stood at the time, becomes Britain's archdruid.

Stukeley's Druidic vision had wide appeal, and other people soon took it in different directions. Architect John Wood, who designed a street intersection in the city of Bath to resemble the layout of Stonehenge, claimed that the Druids had come from ancient Greece and that the monument had been both a Druid college and a temple to the goddess Diana. Dr. John Smith proposed the idea, somewhat ahead of its time, that Stonehenge was a "grand orrery," or a model of the solar system, where the "Arch-Druid standing in his staff"[45] could study movements of the sun, moon, and stars.

The public embraced the idea of Druids as the builders of Stonehenge but largely ignored their proposed roles as wise judge-priests, moon worshipers, or astronomers. Instead, it seized on the darker side of Druidism—maidens sacrificed under a full moon in mysterious rites lit by flickering torches or an eerily glowing bonfire. The large stone near the entrance to the Avenue became the Slaughter Stone where victims were killed and their bodies prepared for burning on the Altar Stone.

Romanticism

Once more, the image of Stonehenge would be one that fit the feelings of the time rather than the evidence of science. The so-called Age of Enlightenment, in which people sought an understanding of the world through logic and reason, was giving way to Romanticism, with its emphasis on emotion and imagination. Artists such as John Constable

An Artist's View

The romantic view of Stonehenge as a Druid temple in which mysterious rites had taken place fueled an interest among artists and writers that began in the 1800s and has continued to the present. One of the more modern interpreters of Stonehenge was the sculptor Henry Moore.

Moore did a series of lithographs of the monument in 1974. He arrived in the Salisbury area late in the evening, intending to go to Stonehenge the next day. Eventually, however, his curiosity got the better of him, as he related in this letter quoted in *The Making of Stonehenge* by

Rodney Castledean:

After eating I decided I wouldn't wait to see Stonehenge until the next day. As it was a clear evening I got to Stonehenge and saw it by moonlight. I was alone and tremendously impressed. (Moonlight as you know enlarges everything, and the mysterious depths and distances made it seem enormous.) I began doing the album as etchings, and only later decided lithographs would be better. Etchings are done with a point making a fine line. The technique isn't a natural one of representing the texture of stone. Also, blackness is more natural to lithography, and the night, the moonlight idea, was more possible.

A photograph captures the beauty of Stonehenge illuminated by moonlight.

and J.M.W. Turner painted Stonehenge as something brooding darkly on a lonely plain as thunderclouds rear their heads in the background and lightning flashes overhead. Others such as Thomas Cole painted idyllic scenes with simple shepherds sitting on fallen stones as their flocks grazed nearby.

Writers followed suit. Poet William Wordsworth wrote about:

> Pile of Stone-henge! so proud to hint yet keep
> Thy secrets, thou that lov'st to stand and hear
> The Plain resounding to the whirlwind's sweep,
> Inmate of lonesome Nature's endless year.[46]

And novelist Thomas Hardy, in a memorable scene from *Tess of the d'Urbervilles,* describes the heroine and her lover taking refuge in Stonehenge at night until the dawn showed "the eastward pillars . . . blackly against the light, and the great flame-shaped Sunstone beyond them; and the Stone of Sacrifice midway."[47]

As a result of such treatments, Druidic ruins became all the rage. Almost any ancient stone structure, man-made or not, became a work of the Druids. And, if stone structures were not immediately at hand, people built them. Many a country home had Stonehenge look-alikes. One wealthy landowner, William Danby, constructed a mock Stonehenge far to the north in Yorkshire and even installed a bearded hermit to add to the effect.

The Tourists Arrive

Stonehenge itself, the lonely monument on the plain, was lonely no longer. It enjoyed a boom of tourism that has never abated. An enterprising carpenter from Amesbury set up a hut against one of the trilithon uprights and "attended there daily with liquors, to entertain the traveler, and show him the stones."[48] And many visitors, having come to see such wonders as the Heel Stone, Slaughter Stone, and Altar Stone, brought hammers with them to break off pieces as souvenirs much to Stukeley's dismay.

Stukeley's romantic view of Stonehenge as a Druid temple had, in Chippindale's words, "cast Stonehenge under a fog-bank of mystification which lasted a century."[49] Indeed, the fog has never entirely lifted. Modern-day Druids by the thousands gather each year at the summer solstice to celebrate.

In part, the Druidic picture became so firmly etched in the public mind because there was little to erase it. Some investigation was done in the 1800s, but little light was shed on the monument's mysteries. It would not be until the 1900s that modern science, with advanced techniques, would begin to lift the veil that Aubrey, Stukeley, and their colleagues had draped over Stonehenge.

Chapter 5

The Archaeologists

The romantic view of Stonehenge as a temple of the Druids held firm throughout the 1800s and well into the twentieth century. Little by little, however, archaeologists using increasingly modern technology began to chip away at the prevailing vision. Working patiently, building on the findings of their predecessors, they coaxed Stonehenge to reveal at least some of its secrets.

It took a dramatic event to rouse the archaeological community to begin reexamining Stonehenge. On January 3, 1797, farmers working in fields half a mile away felt the ground under their feet jolt. The southwest trilithon had fallen outward, its lintel coming to rest against a sarcen of the outer circle. Water had pooled around one of the uprights, worked its way into cracks around the base, froze, then thawed rapidly, thus weakening the entire structure.

Antiquarians flocked to the site, including amateur William Cunnington, a wool merchant from nearby Heyetesbury. Cunnington had become an avid collector of fossils and ancient artifacts. Sponsored by the Reverend William Coxe, he dug into dozens of barrows in the area and started his work at Stonehenge in 1802. Coxe wanted Cunnington to supervise the restoration of the fallen stones, but the owner of Stonehenge, the marquis of Queensberry, refused.

Cunnington would work at Stonehenge and the surrounding countryside until his death in 1810. One of his early discoveries was the hole in which the Slaughter Stone had clearly stood. This signified that the stone had not lain flat, as previously thought, thus deflating the notion of sacrifices having taken place there. More important from the standpoint of dating the monument, however, was his work among the barrows.

A Higher Antiquity

In one of the barrows, just to the west of the monument, Cunnington found a large clay urn that had been used for a cremation. Later, digging by the Altar Stone, he found fragments of similar pottery. Since the barrows were known to predate the coming of the Romans, the discovery of barrow-era pottery at Stonehenge was a further indication that it was also pre-Roman. Also in the barrows were chips of both sarcen and bluestone, from which Cunnington deduced that fragments of the stones from the building of Stonehenge had been lying around the plain when the barrows were constructed. This, he wrote, "gives higher antiquity to our British Temple than many Antiquaries are disposed to allow."[50]

Cunnington's work was eventually published by another of his sponsors, Sir Richard Colt Hoare, in his book *The Ancient History of Wiltshire*. It is a reasoned, factual listing of Cunnington's findings. The Druids are mentioned, but there is nothing that links them with Stonehenge. The monument is pre-Roman, but Cunnington and Colt Hoare can say nothing more definite.

The system that would finally enable scientists to date Stonehenge with at least some accuracy was proposed in 1819 by Christian Jürgen Thomsen of Denmark. Thomsen divided prehistoric times into three divisions according to what tools were used—first stone, then bronze, and finally

Sacrifice at Stonehenge?

Much of the mystery at Stonehenge over the centuries has involved its supposed use by the ancient Druids as a place for religious rites that involved human sacrifice. Just when it appeared that modern science had discounted such grisly stories, however, evidence to the contrary was discovered.

In 1978 archaeologists were excavating the area of the ditch a few feet to the west of the Avenue when they discovered the skeleton of a young man. He had been killed with arrows and his body dumped in the ditch and covered over. Radiocarbon dating showed that he had been killed about 2310 B.C.

Three arrowheads were found among his ribs. Their points were broken off, indicating he had been shot with great velocity from close range. One of the shots had been into his side, one into the chest, and the third from behind.

He was wearing a slate wrist guard, showing that he was an archer. He was much taller (five feet, ten inches) than the other people of that time whose bodies have been found near Stonehenge. Possibly he was an enemy fleeing from some battle.

Another possibility is that the Stonehenge archer had been a prisoner and was murdered as part of a religious sacrifice. The date of his death would fit with that thought to be the time the Avenue was built, so perhaps the young archer was meant to be an offering to the gods to consecrate the new construction.

Whatever the reason for the Stonehenge archer's execution, it had nothing to do with Druids. They did not come to Britain until many centuries later.

Arrowheads similar to these were discovered in 1978 lodged in the ribs of an ancient murder victim.

iron. The Bronze and Iron Ages could be dated in some civilizations, such as Egypt, which had written records, so it was reasonable to think that the presence or absence of such tools could date ancient sites elsewhere.

Lubbock's Work

In 1865 Sir John Lubbock applied this system to Stonehenge. In reviewing Cunnington's notes, he found that of the 151 barrows near the monument, 2 contained iron (found to have been inserted later), 39 had bronze objects, and 110 had no metal at all. If the barrows were indeed older than Stonehenge, this dated the building at least to the Bronze Age (about 1200 to 1000 B.C.) and probably earlier—"a more ancient period than even our most imaginative antiquaries have yet ventured to suggest."[51]

With help from William Cunnington's notes, Sir John Lubbock deduced that Stonehenge was built prior to the Bronze Age.

Many of the experts of the time refused to acknowledge such an early date. They could not believe barbarians who did not even have a written language could build anything like Stonehenge. Some even said, despite all evidence to the contrary, that Stonehenge represented an attempt to build in the Roman manner after the Romans had departed about A.D. 450.

Others still clung to the notion that if Stonehenge were pre-Roman, it must have been built by someone other than the Britons. Like writers in earlier centuries, they tried to find similar monuments in other parts of the world that they could somehow link to Stonehenge. The only places where squared-off trilithons existed were in Mycenae (the ancient Troy) in modern Turkey and near Tripoli in northern Africa. This Mediterranean influence revived the idea of a Phoenician-built Stonehenge.

The overwhelming opinion, however, remained with the Druids, and the second half of the 1800s would provide little to change it. Certainly nothing was to be learned from the structure itself. Ownership of the site had passed in 1824 from the marquis of Queensberry to Sir Edmund Antrobus. After an excavation in front of the Altar Stone in 1839 turned up nothing more significant than rabbit bones, Sir Edmund refused all requests, including all those from the learned societies and proposals to raise fallen stones. As a result, Stonehenge was saved for future generations of investigators.

A Storm of Protest

It took another violent act of nature to renew investigation. On a stormy New Year's Eve in 1900, a sarcen upright on the west side of the outer circle blew down. Its lintel crashed down also, breaking in half on impact. Sir Edmund decided that he would have experts check the security of the remaining stones, build a fence around the monument, and charge admission.

His decision caused an uproar. Archaeologists were afraid the site would be damaged if the stones were restored. A local government council protested that the roads crossing the site should remain open. The National Trust, dedicated to preserving historical sites, argued that Stonehenge was a national treasure and should remain open and free. Sir Edmund stood firm, and a court confrmed his rights.

He did, however, call in experts to check the remaining stones. They found that the remaining upright of the Great Trilithon, which had been increasingly leaning for many years, was in danger of cracking and falling. The man who headed the project of putting it upright was Professor William Gowland, an authority on ancient mining and metalwork.

Gowland had never before done excavation, but his precise methods were far ahead of their time. He dug only in a thirteen-by-seventeen-foot area around the base of the stone, but he took great pains to record everything he found. Before starting, he stretched twine across the area at six-inch intervals. Every artifact was listed by the position and depth at which it had been found. Workers sifted all dirt through meshes to capture the smallest articles.

When the southwest trilithon had fallen in 1797, observers were able to see for the first time, that very little of the uprights' length was actually below the surface. Gowland learned how they had been erected in this manner. One side of each of the holes he excavated was slanted outward instead of being vertical. The uprights had been maneuvered into these ramps, pulled upright, then packed into place.

Raising the Lintels

It was Gowland who proposed that the stones had been transported to Stonehenge on sledges. Furthermore, he suggested that the enormous lintels had been raised into place by placing them on timber frames, then using levers

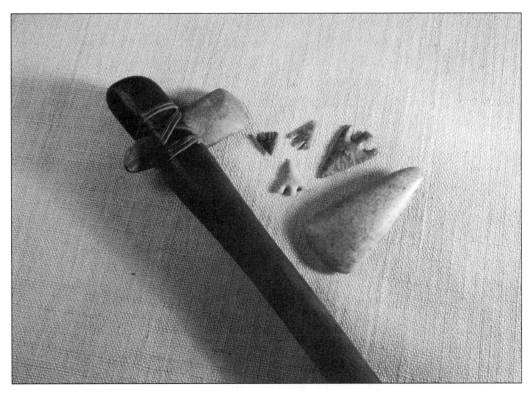

to raise one end and then the other, placing logs underneath each end at every step. In this way, the lintel would slowly rise to the top of the uprights, from where it could slide into place. Other methods have been suggested, including pulling the lintel up an earthen ramp, but none makes more sense than Gowland's.

William Gowland discovered stone tools like these at Stonehenge and estimated that the monument was built in the late Neolithic age.

He also discovered that the bluestone just inside the trilithon upright had been placed into the rubble that had been used to secure the upright and with which the upright's hole had been filled. This proved that the bluestones had been erected after the sarcens, counter to most opinions.

Even more important, Gowland found in the holes only stone tools and fragments of the deer antlers that had been used to hack out the chalk. Only one faint green stain, a remnant of some copper or bronze scrap, hinted at the use of metal. From this, he concluded that Stonehenge had been built "during the latter part of the Neolithic [late stone] age, or the period of transition from stone to bronze, and before that metal had passed into general use."[52] The date he estimated was 1800 B.C., more than one thousand years before either the Druids or the Romans.

Stonehenge finally came under government control during World War I. Sir Edmund was killed without an heir, and his estate was auctioned. A local landowner, Cecil Chubb, bought Stonehenge and three years later gave it to the nation and was knighted for his generosity.

Between the Wars

The years between the world wars were not very kind to Stonehenge. The Office of Works wanted to restore any of the stones in danger of falling and turned to the Society of Antiquaries for advice. The society's president, Sir Arthur Evans, expanded the plan of action to include "an eventual exploration of the whole monument within and including the circular bank and ditch."[53] In other words, he planned to excavate the entire site.

Gowland was originally supposed to supervise, but because he was in failing health, the job went to his assistant, Colonel William Hawley. Hawley was an experienced excavator but lacked Gowland's imagination and was hesitant to link his discoveries with one another and draw conclusions.

The dangerously leaning stones, all on the outer circle, were righted during 1919 to 1920, but the society lacked the money to restore those that had fallen in 1797 and 1900. It did, however, sponsor Hawley's work on the site through 1926. Assisted by R.H. Newall, he systematically dug up most of the entire southern and eastern half of the site, including the ditch. Although Hawley was careful to label and keep everything he found, the collection became so large that he eventually buried everything he considered

Criticism of Hawley

Although Colonel William Hawley made several important discoveries at Stonehenge in the 1920s, modern archaeologists have criticized his method of complete excavation. In his book *Stonehenge,* Richard Atkinson wrote that Hawley

> was obsessed with the danger, or at least the undesirability, of framing any specific questions to be answered by excavation. As a consequence, he continued the mechanical and largely uncritical stripping of the site far beyond the point at which his work ceased to yield significant information. This process, coupled with a regrettable inadequacy in his methods of recording his finds and observations and, one suspects, an insufficient appreciation of the destructive characteristics of excavation *per se,* has left for subsequent excavators a most lamentable legacy of doubt and frustration. For it is now clear that there are a number of problems connected with the history of Stonehenge which it will never be possible to solve by excavation in the future, because the evidence has already been totally destroyed without record of its nature or significance.

unimportant—exactly where, no one knows. His work therefore virtually ruined half the site for future scientists.

Some valuable discoveries were made. Newall persuaded Hawley to follow up on the "cavities" that Aubrey reported in the 1700s. Probing with a steel bar, they discovered the fifty-six holes evenly spaced in a circle. Twenty-one were excavated, turning up cremated bones and flint tools, again pointing to an origin before the Bronze Age. They also discovered the Y and Z holes, which they thought had been dug much later. None of the holes seemed to have held any uprights.

The Bluestones' Origin

Other important discoveries about Stonehenge were made far from the structure itself. In 1923, Dr. H.H. Thomas of the British Geological Survey solved at long last the mystery of the bluestones. They had come, as Geoffrey of Monmouth had written eight hundred years earlier, from far to the west, but from Wales instead of Ireland. In the Preseli Mountains, located in far southwest Wales, a few miles from the Irish Sea and about 140 miles from Stonehenge, Thomas found all three varieties of bluestone that had been used in the monument.

The bluestones could have been transported using a variety of routes, two of them more likely than the rest. The first would skirt the southern Welsh coast, crossing the Severn River estuary and then going up the "Bristol" Avon River (many rivers in England are named Avon, from an old Celtic word), overland to the Wylye River, and up a small stretch of the Hampshire Avon to Stonehenge. The other route, longer but involving less overland travel, would go clear around Saint David's Head—the far southwestern tip of England—to the Hampshire Avon, then up to Stonehenge.

However they were transported, why the builders brought stones from so far away remains a mystery. Some of the bluestone uprights at Stonehenge show signs of having once been lintels, suggesting they were once part of another structure. Perhaps Geoffrey's account of the Giants' Ring had some grain of truth.

In the 1930s speculation shifted from the west to the east. Professor Stuart Piggott wrote about what he called the "Wessex" culture in southern England, where graves had been found that contained gold, bronze, and glass artifacts similar to those from as far away as Egypt. He linked these early Bronze Age relics to similar finds in Mycenae and concluded that Stonehenge was the creation of some unknown architect from the eastern Mediterranean who somehow wound up in Britain.

Research Resumes

Whether Piggott's theory was correct or not would have to wait more than twenty years, until serious archaeological research resumed at Stonehenge under the direction of Piggott, J.F.S. Stone, and Richard Atkinson. Their work, which would continue through the 1950s, would at long last solve many—but not all—of Stonehenge's mysteries.

These archaeologists worked on a very small scale, nothing like the wholesale excavations of Hawley. They had the advantage, however, of a far more powerful tool than the spade. In 1947, American chemist Willard Libby had developed radiocarbon dating, a method whereby material from a once-living plant or animal as old as fifty thousand years could be used to determine with reasonable

American chemist Willard Libby, inventor of the radiocarbon dating process, confirmed Gowland's estimates.

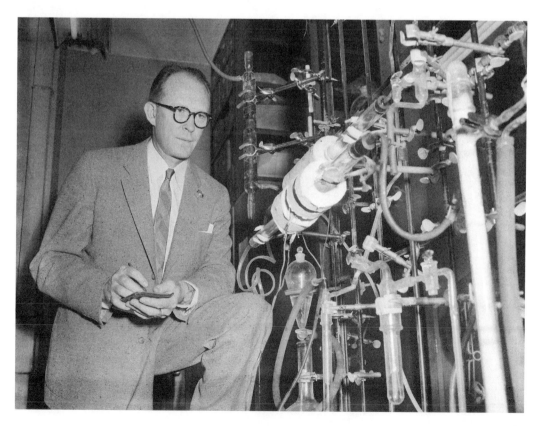

Carvings discovered beneath grafitti similar to this on a trilithon upright confirmed a Mediterranean influence on Stonehenge.

accuracy when the organism had died. A small quantity of carbon 14, a radioactive substance, is present in almost all living matter and, when the organism dies, begins to decay. The age of the organism can be measured by the degree of decay that has taken place.

Piggott, Stone, and Atkinson began their work in 1950, excavating two Aubrey Holes. They found no trace of either a stone upright or a wooden pole, so concluded that the holes had been dug for some unknown purpose. They sent a piece of charcoal from a cremation in one of the holes to Libby, who determined a date of 1848 B.C., plus or minus 275 years. This confirmed Gowland's estimates.

The most dramatic discovery, however, was not under the ground, but had been right in front of observers' eyes all along. In 1953, while photographing some seventeenth-century graffiti on one of the trilithon uprights, Atkinson saw the faint shadow of another carving just below. It was the shape of a dagger similar to those used in ancient Mycenae.

Nearby on the same stone were the outlines of axes of the type that were used in the middle Bronze Age, about 1600–1400 B.C. This seemed to confirm Piggott's theory of a Mediterranean influence on Stonehenge.

The Stages of Stonehenge

By digging in a few key locations and subjecting material—bone, deer antlers, charcoal, wood—to radiocarbon dating, the scientists pieced together the history of Stonehenge. It had not been built at any one time, but in various stages over almost two thousand years.

Atkinson published the findings in his 1956 book *Stonehenge*, claiming that construction had begun about 1800 B.C. In the 1960s, however, corrections in radiocarbon dating showed that it was much older. Suddenly, the starting date of 1800 B.C. became 2600 B.C. or even earlier. The trilithons dated from about 2100 B.C., long before the development of the Mycenaean culture. Therefore, while someone from Mycenae might have carved the dagger and axes, it had been done long after Stonehenge was built.

Atkinson revised his timetable, dividing the building of Stonehenge into four stages. Stonehenge I began somewhere around 3000 B.C. and lasted for about nine hundred years. The builders used deer antler picks to dig the ditch, piling the earth inward to make the six-foot-high bank. Within the bank, fifty-six Aubrey Holes were dug, then filled in. Their exact purpose remains a mystery. The first stone—the Heel Stone—was set up outside the entrance to the northeast and may have had a partner. A large number of holes dating from this period held wooden posts, but no one knows why.

At the start of Stonehenge II (2150–2000 B.C.) the Avenue was begun, a ditch was dug around the Heel Stone, and two stones—one perhaps the Heel Stone's partner—were put up between the Heel Stone and the entrance.

Excavation later showed the entrance had been moved slightly, probably to be more in line with the rising sun at midsummer. The first bluestones arrived and were set up in a half-circle in the Q and R holes. They would eventually be reused elsewhere and the holes filled in. The Station Stones may also date from this period, but that is uncertain.

Stonehenge III

Stonehenge III is usually divided into three overlapping phases. During Stonehenge IIIa, the century right around 2000 B.C., the building of what most people consider the classic Stonehenge took place—the sarcen upright and lintel circle, the trilithons, and the Slaughter Stone and its

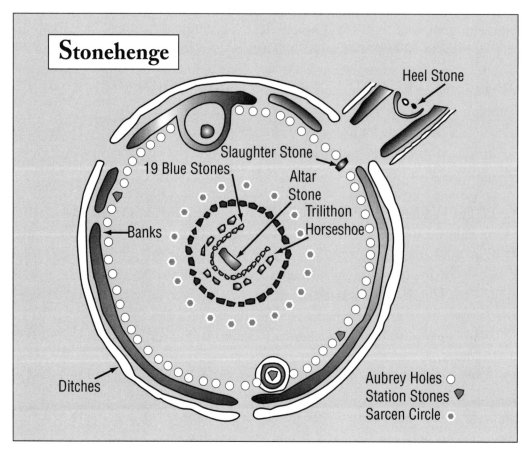

Stonehenge

Heel Stone

Slaughter Stone

19 Blue Stones

Altar Stone

Trilithon Horseshoe

Banks

Ditches

Aubrey Holes ○
Station Stones ▽
Sarcen Circle •

companion in the entrance. The bluestones had been removed, but where they were taken or how many were eventually reused at Stonehenge is not known.

During Stonehenge IIIb (2000–1550 B.C.), bluestones—perhaps some of the same ones as in Stonehenge II—were placed in an oval within the trilithon horseshoe. The Y and Z holes were dug, perhaps to hold other bluestones, but the circles were never completed. The bluestones were reset during Stonehenge IIIc (1550–1100 B.C.) to form a second horseshoe within the trilithons and a circle outside of them.

The work during Stonehenge IV (around 1100 B.C.) was not at the monument but in the Avenue, which was extended from Stonehenge Bottom—a few hundred yards to the northeast—all the way to the Avon River west of Amesbury.

Given the relative uncertainty of radiocarbon dating, archaeologists sometimes quibble over the exact length of each phase, but most agree with the overall scheme. Although some continue to argue otherwise, the work of Atkinson and his colleagues swept away notions of Druids, Romans, Phoenicians, Mycenaeans, or anyone other than the ancient people of Britain. Science had pretty well uncovered the who, when, and how of Stonehenge. The great question—*why*—remained, and Atkinson did not even try to answer it. "There is one short, simple and perfectly correct answer: We do not know, and we shall probably never know."[54]

Many people, however, were unwilling to accept an eternal mystery. They thought the question *why* had an answer—one to be found not in the soil beneath Stonehenge but in the heavens above.

Chapter 6

The Astronomers

Ever since 1740, when William Stukeley observed that the summer solstice sunrise is almost exactly over the Heel Stone when viewed from the center of the Great Trilithon, investigators have tried to label Stonehenge an observatory. They have claimed that the monument was built to study the sun, moon, and planets and to predict their movements. While their evidence has not been conclusive, it at least admits the possibility that the so-called astro-archaeologists have found the answer to Stonehenge's greatest mystery.

The orientation of places of worship to the sun is common to many cultures. Ancient Egyptian temples were built with entrances facing east, as were many Christian cathedrals throughout the Middle Ages. As an 1831 magazine article on Stonehenge claimed, "What can be more probable . . . than that unlettered man in his first worship . . . would direct his attention to that glorious luminary the Sun? . . . the source of his own subsistence."[55]

While most accepted Stonehenge's northeast axis as having something to do with religion, few agreed with Dr. Smith's idea of a "grand orrery." Fewer accepted the opinion of the Reverend Edward Duke, who wrote in 1846 that Stonehenge was one of a group of prehistoric

Sir Norman Lockyear proposed that the Great Trilithon and the Heel Stone (pictured through an opening in the sarcen circle) were erected to reckon the summer solstice.

sites in Wiltshire fashioned into a model of the solar system by "our ingenious ancestors."[56] In 1909, however, Sir Norman Lockyear, a highly respected physicist, revived the idea, claiming the monument had been constructed by "astronomer priests who built and used the ancient temples . . . to mark the sight lines . . . to the places of sunrise and sunset at the chief festivals."[57]

Lockyear's Axis

Lockyear assumed that the Stonehenge builders had aligned the main northeast axis to the exact point where the sun rose at midsummer. If this was true, calculating the monument's

Alignments

Sir Norman Lockyear was one of the first modern scientists to revive the idea of Stonehenge as an ancient astronomical observatory. Writing in 1906, he described how those who built the ancient sites in Britain might have used them and lived at them. This quote is from *Stonehenge and Its Mysteries* by Michael Balfour.

> In a colony of the astronomer-priests who built and used the ancient temples we had of necessity (1) Observations, i.e.; circles in the first place; next something to mark the sight-lines to the clock-star for night work, to the rising of the sun or setting of the warning stars, and to the places of sunrise and sunset at the chief festivals. This something, we have learned, might be another circle, a standing stone, a dolmen [tomb], a cove [small valley], or a holed stone . . . (2) Dwellings which would be many chambered barrows, according to the number of astronomer-priests at the station . . . (3) A water supply for drinking and bathing.

age would be possible. This ability stems from the fact that the sun actually rises in a different location on each summer solstice because of tiny changes in the tilt of the earth's axis. The change is extremely small—only one-seventieth of a degree each hundred years—but can be measured.

Lockyear chose as his main axis a line from the center of the Great Trilithon down the middle of the Avenue. This line, extended farther to the northeast, passes near Sidbury Hill about eight miles away, and Lockyear chose as its terminating point a government surveying mark on the hill. Why he chose this particular point no one knows. There is nothing to connect Sidbury Hill with Stonehenge, from which the hill cannot even be seen.

Using this line, Lockyear calculated that Stonehenge had been built in 1680 B.C. There were, however, several problems with this calculation. First, of course, was the way in which he had rather arbitrarily chosen an axis. Second, there was no way to tell what the builders would have considered the moment of sunrise to be—the first gleam above the horizon, the moment when the entire disk is above the horizon, or a moment when the sun stands exactly over some object such as the Heel Stone.

Lockyear also claimed to be able to date prehistoric monuments by alignments to various stars, but his doubtful methods won him few believers within the scientific community. He nevertheless laid the groundwork for modern astro-archaeology, which was to be applied to Stonehenge later in the century.

Lunar Alignment

The first indication that Stonehenge might have been aligned to the moon as well as to the sun came from Peter Newham, an amateur astronomer. Observers had already noted that lines drawn between the north and west Station Stones and between the south and east Station Stones paralleled the axis of the midsummer sunrise. In 1963 Newham showed that in addition, lines drawn the other way—west to south and north to east—coincided with a line pointing toward the northernmost limit of where the moon rises and sets during its monthly cycle.

These two pairs of lines form an almost perfect rectangle. This is only possible at Stonehenge's latitude—distance north of the equator—because of the position of the moon relative to the earth. Had the monument been built either to the north or south, the lines would not intersect at right angles. Perhaps this was the reason Stonehenge was built where it is.

American astronomer Gerald Hawkins expanded Newham's work. Like Atkinson, Hawkins had a relatively new tool at his disposal, but whereas Atkinson used radiocarbon dating, Hawkins used Harvard University's IBM 7094 computer, which he refers to in his writings as "the machine."

Hawkins and his colleagues plotted the various lines connecting 165 Stonehenge features, including stones, holes, and mounds, to see if there were any significant alignments with the sun, moon, planets, or stars. While none of the lines appeared to track the movement of the stars or planets, the reverse was true for the sun and moon. In his 1965 book *Stonehenge Decoded*, on which he was assisted by John B. White, Hawkins wrote, "I was prepared for some Stonehenge-sun correlation. I was not prepared for the total sun correlation—and I had not at all suspected that there might be almost total moon correlation as well."[58]

Hawkins's Alignments

Scholarship incorporating twentieth-century technology led to the idea that Stonehenge may have been designed as a "Neolithic computer."

Hawkins added alignments to Newham's rectangle, altogether finding thirteen solar and eleven lunar correlations. For example, a line from the north Station Stone to the Heel Stone indicated a spot on the horizon where the moon

would rise at the equinox, or midpoint, of its monthly cycle. As well, a line from the same Station Stone to hole C, one of several irregular holes that Hawley discovered and named A–H, was found to indicate the point of the sunrise at equinox, when day and night are the same length.

Hawkins, however, thought Stonehenge was more than simply an observatory. He called it a "Neolithic computer" and described how the ancient astronomer-priests could predict lunar eclipses. His plan was based on the fact that such eclipses occur over an 18.6-year cycle and that this number multiplied by three is approximately fifty-six, the number of Aubrey Holes. Hawkins showed how a complex system of moving black or white marking stones around the Aubrey Hole circle could tell observers in which year eclipses would happen.

The Stonehenge computer may have been useful in other ways, Hawkins wrote. In addition to predicting eclipses, these alignments

> made a calendar, particularly useful to tell the time for planting crops; they helped to create and maintain priestly power, by enabling the priest to call out the multitude to see the spectacular risings and settings of the sun and moon, most especially the midsummer sunrise over the heel stone and midwinter sunset through the great trilithon, and possibly they served as an intellectual game.[59]

Hawkins's work demonstrated once again the seeming power of Stonehenge to fashion impressions of itself according to the mind-set of the observer and the time of observation. Just as the first glimmer of the sun near the Heel Stone ushers in summer, the mid-1960s were the dawning years of the computer age. Hawkins and others saw computers as powerful new tools capable of solving almost any problem, including such mysteries as those of

Stonehenge. Such thinking may well have colored their judgment, leading them to seek evidence that Stonehenge had been a similar tool for ancient Britons.

Criticism of Hawkins

Hawkins's book enjoyed great popular success. The idea of astronomer-priests looking down the Avenue for the first gleam of dawn recalled the long-held and, by many, not yet relinquished visions of Druids. Many of his fellow scientists, however, had doubts. Atkinson was especially critical in his article "Moonshine on Stonehenge." He pointed out that some of the A–H holes were rough, irregular in shape, and contained no evidence that they had been dug by humans. Also, whereas Hawkins had claimed that the odds of so many alignments occurring by chance was less than one in a million, Atkinson calculated the odds at little less than even. Finally, part of Hawkins's findings depended on alignments between the Station Stones and Aubrey Holes. Since the Station Stones stood atop filled-in Aubrey Holes, it is very possible the two did not exist at the same time and thus could not have been used for an alignment.

Other critics wondered, if the number fifty-six was crucial to the astronomical function of Stonehenge, why none of the many other ancient sites had a similar number of holes or stones. Finally, some of Hawkins's alignments that were supposed to point to the same spot on the horizon, indicating the same solar or lunar event, deviated from one another by as much as two degrees.

Fred Hoyle

As the controversy spread throughout the scientific community, the editor of a respected journal, *Antiquity*, sought help from Fred Hoyle. Hoyle, a professor of astronomy at England's Cambridge University who was

known for creative thinking, agreed to study Hawkins's work and to examine Stonehenge on his own. His conclusions, published in 1966, agreed with those of Hawkins, but in a different way.

Astronomy professor Fred Hoyle discovered that Stonehenge could be used to predict the exact day of a lunar eclipse.

Hoyle agreed that Stonehenge could have been used to predict lunar eclipses, but his method involved moving three stones—representing the sun, moon, and one part of the moon's orbit—around the Aubrey Holes at close to their actual rates of travel, thus turning Stonehenge into a model. Hoyle's method improved on Hawkins's in that it did not involve the Station Stones and could predict the day of an eclipse rather than only the year.

Hoyle also offered an explanation of why some of Hawkins's alignments that were supposed to indicate the same phenomenon deviated from one another. Hoyle said this might have been done deliberately so that the ancient astronomers could have taken the average between the two.

Hoyle accepted the idea that Stonehenge I had been something like Hawkins's computer. The idea was revolutionary in that it overturned ideas about the abilities of the ancient Britons. This view of Stonehenge, Hoyle wrote, "demands a level of intellectual attainment orders of magnitude higher than the standard to be expected from a community of primitive farmers."[60]

If, however, the ancient Britons were so advanced, why did the dozens of other stone circles not show evidence of astronomical use? As one scientist was to show, they did.

Alexander Thom

Alexander Thom, a professor of engineering at Oxford University, had been studying ancient megaliths long before the Stonehenge controversy flared. He found several instances at sites other than Stonehenge where alignments from monuments to points on the horizon corresponded to solar or lunar events.

Thom had also discovered that the British stone circles had been built to common units of length, the megalithic fathom (5.44 feet) and the megalithic yard (2.72 feet). This implied that the ancient Britons had some standard measures, decided on and maintained by a central authority. In addition, he carefully studied the geometry of the megaliths and found six basic shapes that were common to almost all of them.

Thom began his work at Stonehenge in 1973. He agreed that the main northeast axis had been designed along the midsummer sunrise, but that the point of reference was not the Heel Stone, but a small earthen mound—"Peter's Mound," named after Peter Newham. Likewise, he

The northwest trilithon, along with three of its components, form a near-perfect ellipse, a shape that describes the lunar orbit.

rejected Hawkins's lunar lines between various stones and holes as being too short for accuracy. Instead, he proposed other points on the horizon—barrows and hills—as possible markers for lunar events.

Thom also analyzed Stonehenge's geometry. He found that the outer sarcen circle was indeed a true circle and that four of the five trilithons—the Great Trilithon being the exception—had been arranged in a near-perfect ellipse.

Thom's findings were well received. Even Atkinson was impressed, conceding that Stonehenge might, after all, have been used to forecast eclipses. Such a concession became all the more dramatic when the recalibration of radiocarbon dates shoved back the building of Stonehenge I—which probably contained most of the stones and holes used for astronomical predictions—another thousand years. As a modern observer, Rodney Castledean writes, "Our ancestors' knowledge of geometry, if what Thom says is true, was at a level that would not be attained again anywhere in Europe until the time of the mathematicians of ancient Greece"[61] 2,000 years later.

Remaining Problems

Still, there were problems with the ideas that Hawkins, Hoyle, and Thom set forth. If Stonehenge and the other megaliths were used for astronomical observation, why has no evidence of record keeping—such as carvings on the stones—ever been found? Also, some of the horizon markers that Thom found turned out to be either too early or too late (one was a military bunker from the 1600s) to have been used at Stonehenge. Even Peter's Mound proved to be a twentieth-century garbage dump. Moreover, with so many megaliths containing so many stones and so many holes and so many various points on the horizon, the likelihood increases that any significant alignment will be a matter of pure chance.

The astronomers have never succeeded in proving that Stonehenge was an observatory or astronomical calculator, only in showing that it might have been. Their research has forced the scientific community—even reluctant archaeologists—to admit that much. Perhaps the mistake that astronomers and archaeologists alike made was trying, once again, to force the round peg of Stonehenge into the square hole of modern science. If the monument was used for astronomy at all, it was not astronomy in the present sense, with its advanced mathematics and high degree of technical accuracy. The ancient Britons would not have been interested in the sun and moon as mathematical abstractions, but in a religious sense having to do with seasons and crops. As Castledean writes, "We must be beware of peopling prehistory with ourselves, thinly disguised."[62]

When the dust of the scientific furor settled, the answer to the primary mystery of why Stonehenge was built remained just as before: We do not know. Since it is an open question, however, speculation has, if anything, increased. And, as computer age has yielded to New Age, that speculation has spun off down many far different roads to sometimes bizarre conclusions.

Chapter 7

New Age, New Druids, New Theories

Just as air rushes to fill a vacuum, explanations of all kinds come from all directions, attempting to answer questions science has been unable to fathom. When experts like Richard Atkinson admit that we may never know the purpose for Stonehenge, they leave, as John Fowles wrote in *The Enigma of Stonehenge*, "a huge empty space, a field for speculation, in the less scientific mind." The spaces, however, are soon filled with "theories about them, however nonsensical, however rationally and statistically improbable."[63]

Proponents of many of these theories are following the time-honored tradition of interpreting Stonehenge in light of their own views. Many are people who have turned against modern science in favor of the so-called New Age philosophy incorporating spiritualism and natural environmental forces. They may, like writer William Irwin Thompson, dismiss scientists as "geniuses with trivia and ignoramuses with ideas" who are "unconscious apologists [defenders] for industrial civilization."[64]

Mainstream scientists have responded with reactions varying from amused tolerance to outright scorn. Archaeologist Christopher Chippindale, while discounting the validity of most of the newer theories, nevertheless considers them valuable in that they maintain a view about Stonehenge "not as an artifact tamed by our own age but as a sacred place."[65] Atkinson, however, considers most of the nontraditional theories to be "the product of that lunatic fringe of archaeology to which Stonehenge has always acted, and still acts, as an irresistible magnet."[66]

Most of the alternative views are not new, but instead have their roots in antiquity. This is natural enough, since the New Age philosophy looks back to a time before science attempted to find exact causes and effects for every phenomenon, back to a time when humanity was supposedly more in

It still remains unclear whether Stonehenge was built as an astronomical observatory, a commemorative monument, sacred site, UFO, or other artifact.

tune with nature and the environment. The alternative views attempt to look at Stonehenge not as a single monument, but as part of a giant cosmic plan.

The Modern Druids

The most persistent of these theories—that the Druids built Stonehenge—certainly is nothing new. Indeed, despite all scientific evidence to the contrary, the theory has endured ever since Aubrey and Stukeley first proposed it. The chief proponents of this view are the Druids themselves—not the ancient British priests, but the members of the Ancient Order of Druids, founded in 1781 as a secret fraternal society.

The Druid Perspective

When the British government moved to restrict access by modern-day Druids and others to Stonehenge at the midsummer solstice, there was widespread protest. One man, Sid Rawle, who had led a group of squatters wishing to camp at Stonehenge, wrote this letter to the *Times* of London, which is quoted in *The Making of Stonehenge* by Rodney Castledean

We come to Stonehenge because in an unstable world it is proper that the people should look for stability to the past in order to learn for the future. . . . The evidence is indisputable that Stonehenge and the surrounding area is one of the most powerful spiritual centers in Europe. It is right that we should meekly stand in the presence of God, but it is proper that we should sing and dance and shout for joy for the love and mercy that He shows us. . . . We would not run a road through Stonehenge and given our way it would soon be removed. A very important part of the monument is now a tarmac car park, ugly to behold. We would not surround it with barbed wire and arc lamps. . . . The Director-General [of the National Trust] will know that he and he alone is all that stands between the festival at present and what he would call a legal festival. . . . Holy land is holy land and our right to be upon it cannot be denied.

Even though the modern Druids do not claim to practice the same prehistoric rites—after all, no one knows with any degree of certainty what they were—they nevertheless claim kinship with their ancient counterparts. It is natural enough, then, that they sought out Stonehenge as a sacred site.

As for the archaeological evidence that Stonehenge predates the ancient Druids by hundreds of years, the modern Druids contend that perhaps there were "proto-Celts" who came to Britain from mainland Europe as early as 2000 B.C. and who could have built Stonehenge. They can offer little explanation, however, why the ancient priests would have abandoned their stone circles and conducted worship in groves of trees. Instead, like so many others, they take what few clues exist and fashion a theory to fit their image of Stonehenge.

The 1905 Initiation

The first modern Druid ceremony at the monument took place in 1905. More than 600 members made the trip to the Wiltshire plain to take part in the initiation of 256 new members. As policemen kept a large crowd of curious onlookers at a distance, the initiates walked blindfolded between two lines of Druids dressed in long white robes, each one wearing a long white false beard and holding a ceremonial sickle. After the newcomers swore an oath, their blindfolds were removed and they were greeted with a song:

> See, see the flames arise!!
> Brothers now your songs prepare!
> And ere their vigour droops and dies
> Our mysteries let him share![67]

The mysteries of the modern-day Druids doubtless contain nothing sinister. Rather the group is an organization much like the Freemasons or other fraternal orders. While maintaining secret rites, they exist largely for fellowship and to undertake philanthropic works.

The 1905 initiation was significant, however, in that it paved the way for future ceremonies. The Druids claimed Stonehenge as their sacred ground, even burying part of the ashes of deceased members there. Eventually, they moved their ceremonies to coincide with the summer solstice in June. In 1920, they tried to expand their service to four days, but the Office of Public Works refused, saying that "some limit must be set to this absurd and degrading nonsense."[68]

The Celebrations Expand

Eventually, objections were overcome and the Druid ceremonies at Stonehenge continued, even though the members sometimes complained about having to pay admission like everyone else. Their rites, however, drew not only more members but also more onlookers, and the midsummer event took on a circuslike atmosphere. Increasingly, especially during the 1960s, the Druids had to compete with hippies, rock musicians, self-proclaimed witches, antiwar demonstrators, sun worshipers, drug dealers, and the merely curious.

Officials tried to limit access inside the monument to the Druids, using police and eventually barbed wire to hold others back. In 1969, however, a crowd estimated at two thousand poured over the wire to have its own celebration. The crowds grew larger and more rowdy until, in 1985, the National Trust, which owns Stonehenge, and English Heritage, which operates it, cracked down, prohibiting all visitors on the solstice and blocking roads to the monument. A violent confrontation took place, and 520 would-be pilgrims were arrested.

After a few years, visitors were allowed back at Stonehenge at midsummer, but not given access to the monument itself. Instead, the Druids and others held their celebrations—far smaller and more peaceful than before—outside the fence.

The Circle Reopened

Thus encouraged, officials agreed in 2000 to make the interior of Stonehenge open to the public at midsummer on a trial basis for the first time in sixteen years. Despite cloudy, rainy weather, about six thousand people showed up.

Few problems arose, so the monument was opened again for the 2001 solstice. Again, the crowd was peaceful, despite being twice as large as the year before. Police reported only five arrests among the fourteen thousand people.

Midsummer morning was cloudy once more in 2002, but that did not stop more than twenty-three thousand people from descending on Stonehenge. Even though disappointed in not being able to see the sunrise, the crowd was well behaved. Only eleven arrests were recorded, all for minor drug and alcohol violations, and a few dozen people were ejected for trying to climb on the stones.

A group of hippies dances at Stonehenge. The monument has also become a gathering place for modern Druids and witches.

Rolo Maughling, an archdruid from the city of Glastonbury, told a local newspaper, "It was wonderful right from the start. There were thousands of people, full of enthusiasm, and everyone has been beautifully behaved. There was a very good spiritual vibration in the stones all night."[69]

Other Views

The Druids, however, are not alone in going back centuries to find inspiration for theories that challenge the findings of science. Several modern views spring from the idea that Stonehenge cannot be properly examined standing alone, but as part of a grand plan that encompasses other prehistoric sites both in Britain and throughout the world.

The linking of Stonehenge with other sites goes all the way back to Geoffrey of Monmouth and his tale of Merlin

Despite uncooperative weather, over 23,000 people descended upon Stonehenge in 2002 to view the summer solstice.

bringing the stones from the Giants' Ring in Ireland. The first mention of a purposeful connection seems to have been Dr. John Smith's claim in 1771 that Stonehenge combines with other sites to form an orrery, or model of the solar system.

In the mid-1800s, Dr. Edward Duke said that sites along a sixteen-mile straight line, including Stonehenge, represented the planets. If these temples could move, he said, they would revolve around Silbury Hill, not to be confused with Sidbury Hill, which is much closer to Stonehenge. He did not venture an opinion on what good a stationary model would have done the builders.

Sir Norman Lockyear, who proposed an astronomical alignment between Stonehenge and nearby Sidbury Hill in the early 1900s, also thought it was somehow significant that his line, if extended southwest, passed through the Iron Age hill fort of Grovely Castle. He also noted that lines drawn from Grovely Castle to Stonehenge to Old Sarum, an ancient site just north of Salisbury, form an equilateral triangle.

The Ley Concept

Such observations led in the twentieth century to the concept of leys. Photographer Alfred Watkins coined the word in 1921, describing them as "a network of lines, standing out like glowing wires all over the surface of the country, intersecting at the sites of churches, old stones, and other spots of traditional sanctity."[70] According to Watkins, leys were marked out by ancient surveyors, ever since which people, knowingly or not, have constructed religious sites—from Stonehenge to modern churches—along them.

The most famous ley passing through Stonehenge is called the Old Sarum Ley. It runs south from the center of the monument, through a well at the center of the site of the abandoned medieval town of Old Sarum, through Salisbury Cathedral, just past a ruined medieval chapel, then on to two prehistoric hill forts, Clearbury Ring and Frankenbury Camp.

Another well-known line, the Stonehenge Ley, follows Lockyear's famous axis. It begins at the Castle Ditches hill fort and extends northeast through Grovely Castle, across a barrow, through Stonehenge and along the Avenue, across the edge of Sidbury Hill, and across two more barrows, ending at an old crossroads.

One writer, Paul Screeton, claimed that leys represent "a striking network of lines of subtle force across Britain, and elsewhere on spaceship Earth, understood and marked in prehistoric times by men of wisdom and cosmic consciousness."[71] Their exact purpose is not made clear, except that perhaps they possess some mystical power from which the sites built on them draw their holiness.

Others have extended the idea of leys far beyond Britain, finding lines connecting sites throughout the world. This has, in turn, fueled speculation that these supposed lines of power were laid out by some extraterrestrial force. As far back as 1972, a man named Waltire, whose first name has been lost, noted that many ancient British monuments appear to have been built to be seen from the air.

Stonehenge as UFO?

More recently, John Michell, in one of his many books on unexplained phenomena, speculates that alien beings in flying saucers may have visited Earth thousands of years ago, making such an impression on the ancient Britons that they built Stonehenge in a circular shape. The bank and ditch might represent the outer edge; the Aubrey Holes, portholes; the sarcen circle, the cabin; the trilithons, a cockpit; and the smaller bluestones, passengers. Michell wrote that Stonehenge thus might be "a sort of cargo cult monument, a pattern of the sacred disc, built to attract this object for which men felt such a yearning."[72]

The circular form of the ditch has led some to believe that the monument is the work of extraterrestrials.

Such an idea, though it perhaps seems bizarre, has a modern counterpart. During World War II, some South Pacific islanders who had never had contact with modern civilization thought soldiers who alighted from airplanes were gods. When the soldiers had left, the islanders built crude replicas of airplanes out of branches and vines to try to lure the visitors back from the sky.

One of the problems with the ley theory is that an almost infinite number of them can be drawn. Britain has so many prehistoric sites that a straight line from Stonehenge in virtually any direction will pass through several of them. In addition, some of the points along a ley—Salisbury

Cathedral, for example—were located where they were built for reasons that are clearly known and are unrelated to an alignment.

Mystic Numbers

Numbers, as well as lines of force, played major roles in the building of Stonehenge, according to some modern writers. Michell, for instance, has compared the dimensions of Stonehenge to those of the earth. He also proposes that both Stonehenge and Glastonbury Abbey, one of the most sacred spots in medieval England and the supposed burial place of King Arthur, were built on similar numerical systems. The basic number for both, he claims, is 666, the "number of the beast" in the biblical book of Revelation. From this, he concludes that both sites represent New Jerusalem, the heavenly city to come after God's final judgment against the world.

Author John Michell proposed that Glastonbury Abbey and Stonehenge were built using similar sacred numerical systems.

Yet another modern writer, Bonnie Gaunt, puts aside modern evidence, including radiocarbon dating. She links the geometry of Stonehenge and the Great Pyramid in Egypt. For instance, she writes, similar angles can be drawn from both sites, one line of which goes through Jerusalem. She concludes that after the Great Flood described in the biblical story of Noah, God designed both structures and assigned the job of building them to Shem, one of Noah's sons.

Many other theories have crowded their way onto Stonehenge's stage. Guy Underwood, a dowser, or searcher for underground springs, suggests that stones, both upright and prone, have been carefully placed within spaces that are surrounded by a network of such springs. It is this underground water, he writes, that gives the stones their legendary healing power.

Finding the Right Clues

Many of those who advance the so-called alternative theories seem to follow the same pattern as the mainstream scientists before them. They find in Stonehenge exactly what they are looking for. Like Stukeley, who wrote that his theory about the Druids was "reasonable conjecture,"[73] they sift through many clues—alignments, angles, and legends—to find those that will produce the result they seek.

Indeed, one of the mysteries of Stonehenge is that no matter how much is discovered about it, still more questions seem to emerge. As William Hawley put it, "The more we dig, the more the mystery appears to deepen."[74] Stonehenge speaks with many voices, telling listeners exactly what they want to hear, and the listeners are satisfied, thinking they have found the truth. Stonehenge is a tempter, a teaser. It holds out the promise of divulging the answer to its most enduring mystery—that of why it was built—but keeps that answer tantalizingly out of reach. As British prime minister William Gladstone said in 1853, Stonehenge is a relic "telling much and telling that it conceals more."[75]

Epilogue

For Every Season

When British author Samuel Pepys visited Stonehenge in 1668, he was impressed enough to call the stones "prodigious as any tales I ever heard of." He concluded the entry in his diary, "God knows what their use was! they are hard to tell, but yet may be told."[76]

Indeed, the search for the answers to Stonehenge's mysteries continues. Old theories are cast into doubt by new discoveries. The newer theories may yet fall victim to future discoveries. The idea that Stonehenge was the burial site of an ancient British hero had never been supported with evidence. And yet, in May 2002, a tomb was discovered only two miles from the site. The skeleton, dated 2300 B.C., was surrounded by objects—gold earrings, copper knives—that made it clear he was a person of great wealth.

One archaeologist, Dr. Andrew Fitzpatrick, said, "He was possibly the king of the monument because of his obvious status."[77] Was this the chieftain whose wealth and power made the building of the stone circle possible? Was this the man who came down in legend as Aurelius Ambrosius? As usual, there are no answers, only more questions.

Preserving Stonehenge

In the meantime, the more immediate question is how to preserve this monument as it has stood for thousands

The identity of this ancient skeleton exhumed at Stonehenge in 2002 is the latest mystery surrounding the stone circle.

of years. Scientists long have pleaded for the government to close the main highway, the A303, that passes within twelve feet of the Heel Stone. The vibrations from passing trucks, they say, will eventually cause more stones to fall.

The government first proposed constructing a "cut and cover" tunnel that would put the 2 kilometers (1.3 miles) of the highway nearest Stonehenge underground. In October 2001, however, the National Trust proposed instead a tunnel that would be deeper, longer at 4.5 kilometers (2.8 miles), and would take the highway in a long curve around the monument. Such a plan, said National Trust chairman

Charles Nunneley, "is a once-in-a-lifetime opportunity to free Stonehenge of the damaging impact of roads."[78]

If the present highway is removed, it will be done very carefully. Stonehenge has doubtless seen the last of wholesale excavations of the kind that Hawley undertook. Instead, the earth under the highway will be explored inch by inch. Who knows what new discoveries, new clues, and perhaps new riddles will come to light?

New Clues, New Ideas

Whatever they are, certainly they will be interpreted in various ways. It has ever been thus with Stonehenge. Perhaps, in an Internet age, there will be those who claim it is some sort of communication device. Or will there be another discovery, such as the dagger carvings, that rekindle ideas of a link with other ancient civilizations?

Perhaps, as Sir Richard Colt Hoare wrote in 1812, "we may admire; we may conjecture; but we are doomed to remain in ignorance and obscurity."[79] The mysterious stones, while they have told so much, remain silent on so much more. Perhaps that is best. Perhaps humanity should be free to hold on to and treasure its mysteries. Perhaps the ultimate answer to Stonehenge, as poet Siegfried Sassoon writes, is that there is no answer:

> What is Stonehenge? It is the roofless past;
> Man's ruinous myth; his uninterred adoring
> Of the unknown in sunrise cold and red;
> His quest of stars that arch his doomed exploring.
>
> And what is Time but shadows that were cast
> By these storm-sculptured stones while centuries fled?
> The stones remain; their stillness can outlast
> The skies of history hurrying overhead.[80]

Notes

Introduction: The Puzzle on the Plain

1. Quoted in R.J.C. Atkinson, *Stonehenge*. London: Penguin Books, 1979, p. 184.

Chapter One: The Silent Stones

2. Quoted in Christopher Chippindale, *Stonehenge Complete*. London: Thames and Hudson, 1994, p. 40.

Chapter Two: Merlin and Magic

3. Quoted in Chippindale, *Stonehenge Complete*, p. 6.
4. Quoted in Chippindale, *Stonehenge Complete*, p. 21.
5. Quoted in Michael Balfour, *Stonehenge and Its Mysteries*. New York: Charles Scribner's Sons, 1980, p. 11.
6. Quoted in Chippindale, *Stonehenge Complete*, p. 22.
7. Quoted in Chippindale, *Stonehenge Complete*, p. 22.
8. Quoted in Chippindale, *Stonehenge Complete*, p. 24.
9. Quoted in Fernand Neil, *The Mysteries of Stonehenge*. New York: Avon Books, 1974, p. 100.
10. Quoted in Chippindale, *Stonehenge Complete*, p. 25.
11. Quoted in Chippindale, *Stonehenge Complete*, p. 25.
12. Quoted in Chippindale, *Stonehenge Complete*, p. 26.
13. Quoted in Chippindale, *Stonehenge Complete*, p. 26.
14. Quoted in Chippindale, *Stonehenge Complete*, p. 28.
15. Quoted in Chippindale, *Stonehenge Complete*, p. 28.
16. Quoted in Chippindale, *Stonehenge Complete*, p. 42.
17. Quoted in Chippindale, *Stonehenge Complete*, p. 37.
18. Quoted in Chippindale, *Stonehenge Complete*, p. 41.

Chapter Three: Romans, Danes, and Phoenicians

19. William Stukeley, *Stonehenge: A Temple Restor'd to the British Druids*. New York: Garland, 1984. p. 2.
20. Quoted in Rodney Castledean, *The Making of Stonehenge*. London: Routledge, 1993, p. 10.
21. Quoted in Balfour, *Stonehenge and Its Mysteries*, p. 15.
22. Quoted in Balfour, *Stonehenge and Its Mysteries*, p. 16.
23. Quoted in Chippindale, *Stonehenge Complete*, p. 57.
24. Quoted in Chippindale, *Stonehenge Complete*, p. 61.
25. Quoted in Chippindale, *Stonehenge Complete*, p. 60.
26. Quoted in Castledean, *The Making of Stonehenge*, p. 14.

27. Quoted in Chippindale, *Stonehenge Complete*, p. 65.
28. Quoted in Chippindale, *Stonehenge Complete*, p. 28.
29. Quoted in Chippindale, *Stonehenge Complete*, p. 37.
30. Quoted in Chippindale, *Stonehenge Complete*, p. 71.

Chapter Four: Aubrey, Stukeley, and the Druids

31. Quoted in Gerald S. Hawkins and John B. White, *Stonehenge Decoded*. Garden City, NY: Doubleday, 1965, p. 13.
32. Quoted in Balfour, *Stonehenge and Its Mysteries*, p. 20.
33. Quoted in Chippindale, *Stonehenge Complete*, p. 68.
34. Quoted in Chippindale, *Stonehenge Complete*, p. 68.
35. Quoted in Hawkins and White, *Stonehenge Decoded*, p. 13.
36. Quoted in Castledean, *The Making of Stonehenge*, p. 16.
37. Quoted in Chippindale, *Stonehenge Complete*, p. 72.
38. Stukeley, *Stonehenge: A Temple Restor'd*, p. 41.
39. Stukeley, *Stonehenge: A Temple Restor'd*, p. 35.
40. Stukeley, *Stonehenge: A Temple Restor'd*, p. 15.
41. Stukeley, *Stonehenge: A Temple Restor'd*, p. 45.
42. Quoted in Balfour, *Stonehenge and Its Mysteries*, p. 27.
43. Stukeley, *Stonehenge: A Temple Restor'd*, p. 11.

44. Chippindale, *Stonehenge Complete*, p. 41.
45. Quoted in Balfour, *Stonehenge and Its Mysteries*, p. 30.
46. Quoted in Chippindale, *Stonehenge Complete*, p. 98.
47. Quoted in Chippindale, *Stonehenge Complete*, p. 112.
48. Quoted in Chippindale, *Stonehenge Complete*, p. 90.
49. Chippindale, *Stonehenge Complete*, p. 86.

Chapter Five: The Archaeologists

50. Quoted in Chippindale, *Stonehenge Complete*, p. 122.
51. Quoted in Chippindale, *Stonehenge Complete*, p. 156.
52. Quoted in Chippindale, *Stonehenge Complete*, p. 156.
53. Quoted in Chippindale, *Stonehenge Complete*, p. 179.
54. Atkinson, *Stonehenge*, p. 168.

Chapter Six: The Astronomers

55. Quoted in Chippindale, *Stonehenge Complete*, p. 137.
56. Quoted in Castledean, *The Making of Stonehenge*, p. 19.
57. Quoted in Balfour, *Stonehenge and Its Mysteries*, p. 33.
58. Hawkins and White, *Stonehenge Decoded*, p. 107.
59. Hawkins and White, *Stonehenge Decoded*, p. 117.
60. Quoted in Castledean, *The Making of Stonehenge*, p. 26.
61. Castledean, *The Making of Stonehenge*, p. 26.

62. Castledean, *The Making of Stonehenge,* p. 26.

Chapter Seven: New Age, New Druids, New Theories

63. John Fowles, *The Enigma of Stonehenge.* New York: Summit Books, 1980, p. 110.
64. Quoted in Chippindale, *Stonehenge Complete,* pp. 234, 244.
65. Chippindale, *Stonehenge Complete,* p. 249.
66. Atkinson, *Stonehenge,* p. 193.
67. Quoted in Chippindale, *Stonehenge Complete,* p. 173.
68. Quoted in Chippindale, *Stonehenge Complete,* p. 190.
69. Quoted in *This Is Wiltshire,* "Revellers Swamp Stones," June 27, 2002. www.thisiswiltshire.co.uk.
70. Quoted in Chippindale, *Stonehenge Complete,* p. 236.
71. Quoted in Chippindale, *Stonehenge Complete,* p. 238.
72. Quoted in Chippindale, *Stonehenge Complete,* p. 241.
73. Quoted in Chippindale, *Stonehenge Complete,* p. 92.
74. Quoted in Chippindale, *Stonehenge Complete,* p. 183.
75. Quoted in Chippindale, *Stonehenge Complete,* p. 152.

Epilogue: For Every Season

76. Quoted in Balfour, *Stonehenge and Its Mysteries,* p. 19.
77. Quoted in *Bath Chronicle,* "King of Stonehenge," May 16, 2002.
78. Quoted in *Amesbury Journal,* "Trust Calls for Longer Stonehenge Tunnel," October 18, 2001.
79. Quoted in Balfour, *Stonehenge and Its Mysteries,* p. 31.
80. Quoted in Fowles, *The Enigma of Stonehenge,* p. 127.

For Further Reading

Books

Hariette Abels, *Stonehenge*. Mankato, MI: Crestwood House, 1987. Good introduction to Stonehenge for younger readers.

Sheridan Bowman, *Radiocarbon Dating*. Berkeley and Los Angeles: University of California Press, 1990. Part of the Interpreting the Past series published jointly with the British Museum. A description of the radiocarbon technique for the advanced reader.

Franklyn Mansfield Branley, *The Mystery of Stonehenge*. New York: HarperCollins Children's Books, 1969. Good, straightforward examination of the mysteries surrounding Stonehenge and the extent to which they have been solved.

Miranda J. Green, *The World of the Druids*. London: Thames and Hudson, 1997. Examines both the myths and what few facts are actually known about these ancient priests.

James Jesperson and Jane Fitz-Randolph, *Mummies, Dinosaurs, Moon Rocks: How We Know How Old Things Are*. New York: Atheneum Books, 1996. Good explanation of methods of dating, including radiocarbon and tree rings, for younger readers.

Caroline Malone and Nancy Stone Bernard, *Stonehenge*. Oxford, England: Oxford University Press, 2002. Part of the Digging in the Past series. Good summary of both the legends and the scientific research surrounding the monument.

Wendy Mass, *Stonehenge*. San Diego: Lucent Books, 1998. Part of the Building History series. Comprehensive look at the way modern science believes that Stonehenge was built over the centuries.

Websites

The Complete Stonehenge (www.amherst. edu). Highly entertaining website put together by Emily Mace, a student at Amherst College in Massachusetts.

Great Buildings Online (www.greatbuild ings.com). Part of the Great Buildings Online series. Comments on the building of Stonehenge from an architectural perspective.

Stonehenge (http://witcombe.sbc.edu). Excellent description of the phases of Stonehenge's construction, plus some spectacular color pictures.

Works Consulted

Books

R.J.C. Atkinson, *Stonehenge*. London: Penguin Books, 1979. Groundbreaking study of Stonehenge by a master archaeologist whose work answered many of the mysteries as to when it was built.

Michael Balfour, *Stonehenge and Its Mysteries*. New York: Charles Scribner's Sons, 1980. Excellent description of the history of Stonehenge, including explanations of the theories surrounding its construction. Well illustrated with photographs, maps, and diagrams.

Rodney Castledean, *The Making of Stonehenge*. London: Routledge, 1993. Extremely well-researched and detailed account of how and when scientists believe that Stonehenge was built.

Christopher Chippindale, *Stonehenge Complete*. London: Thames and Hudson, 1994. Comprehensive, well-documented, and superbly illustrated account of Stonehenge as it has been viewed by investigators throughout history.

John Fowles, *The Enigma of Stonehenge*. New York: Summit Books, 1980. The well-known novelist describes the many theories as to how Stonehenge was built and why. Lavishly photographed by Barry Brukoff.

Bonnie Gaunt, *Stonehenge: A Closer Look*. Ann Arbor, MI: Braun-Brumfield, 1979. The author draws geometrical comparisons between Stonehenge and the Great Pyramid of Egypt and connects the alignments of stones and holes with biblical events.

Gerald S. Hawkins and John B. White, *Stonehenge Decoded*. Garden City, NY: Doubleday, 1965. Controversial book in which Hawkins, as the primary author, theorizes, based on the alignment of several stones and holes, that Stonehenge was used as an astronomical computer.

Fernand Neil, *The Mysteries of Stonehenge*. New York: Avon Books, 1974. After a thorough discussion of Stonehenge and its proportions, the author concludes that it was the product of an architect not native to Britain.

William Stukeley, *Stonehenge: A Temple Restor'd to the British Druids*. New York: Garland, 1984. Facsimile reprinting of 1740 study on Stonehenge. Also contains Stukeley's 1743 book on Avebury.

Periodicals

Amesbury Journal, "Trust Calls for Longer Stonehenge Tunnel," October 18, 2001.

Bath Chronicle, "King of Stonehenge," May 16, 2002.

Internet Source

This Is Wiltshire, "Revellers Swamp Stones," June 27, 2002. www.thisiswiltshire.co.uk.

Index

Abraham, 55

Africa, 27, 43, 65

Age of Enlightenment, 57

Alfred the Great (Saxon king), 41

aliens, 96

Altar Stone, 15, 17, 57, 59, 62, 65

Amesbury, 52, 59, 75

Ancient History of Wiltshire (Hoare), 62

Ancient Order of Druids, 90

Anglo-Saxons, 15

antiquarians, 22, 40, 43, 61

Antiquaries, Society of, 51, 68

Antiquity (journal), 82

Antrobus, Sir Edmund, 40, 65, 66, 68

archaeological discoveries
  burial site, 23, 69
  garbage dump, 86
  origin of bluestones, 70
  relics and artifacts, 37, 62, 66, 67
  use of radiocarbon dating, 63, 71–72, 73

archaeologists, 61, 63, 66, 71, 86

archdruid, 57

astro-archaeology, 79

astronomer-priests, 78, 81, 82

astronomers, 86

astronomical investigation

alignment with sun and moon, 77-80

eclipses, 81, 83, 86

an observatory, 54, 76

prediction of cropping seasons, 87

solstices, 76, 78, 83, 84

Atkinson, Richard, 69, 71, 72, 73, 75, 79, 82, 86, 88, 89

Aubrey, John, 22, 23, 37, 47, 48, 49, 51, 55, 60, 69, 90

Aubrey holes, 21–22

Aurelius Ambrosius (British king), 27, 28, 29, 30, 31, 34,

Avebury, 12, 13, 45, 48, 51, 56

Avenue, the, 23, 24, 52, 57, 63, 78

Avon River, 31, 45, 70, 75

Balfour, Michael, 78

Bards (former British priests), 49

barrows, 11, 12, 54, 61-62, 96

Bath, 57

Birth of Merlin, The (Rowley), 32

bluestones, 17, 19, 70, 75, 97

Boadicea (British queen), 39

Bolton, Edmund, 39

book of Revelation, 98

Brief Lives (Aubrey), 47

Britain, 11, 13, 25, 29, 36, 39, 43, 47, 49, 54, 63, 75, 78, 91, 95, 96, 98

Britannia Antiqua Ilustrata (Sammes), 49

British Geological Survey, 70

British Isles, 11, 49

Bronze Age, 64, 69, 70

Buckingham, 37

Bulford, 31

Caesar, Julius, 50, 52

Cambridge University, 82

capstone, 12

Castledean, Rodney, 27, 58, 86, 87, 90

Castle Ditches, 96

Caxton, William, 29

Charles II (king of England), 41, 48

Charleton, Walter, 41, 48

Chippindale, Christopher, 14, 16, 30, 49, 56, 60, 89

Christianity, 55

Chubb, Cecil, 68

Church of England, 51, 55, 56

Chyndonax the Druid. *See* Stukeley, William

Cibber, Susannah, 34

Claudius (emperor of Rome), 39

Clearbury Ring, 96

Cole, Thomas, 58

computer age, 87

Constable, John, 57–58
Cornwall, 39
Coxe, William, 61
Cunnington, William, 61,
  62, 64

Danby, William, 59
Danes, 41
Daniel, Samuel, 34
Defoe, Daniel, 14
De Heere, Lucas, 16
Denmark, 43, 62
Devises, 13
Diana (goddess), 57
dolmen (tomb markers), 12
dolomites. *See* bluestones
Druidism, 55, 57
Druids, 49, 50, 51, 55, 57,
  59, 63, 65, 68, 75, 82, 90,
  91, 92, 94, 99
Dryden, John, 41
Duke, Edward, 76, 95
dysser (Danish stone tombs),
  41

Earth, 54, 96
Easton Pierse, 47
eclipse, 81, 83
Egypt, 64, 70, 98
Einstein, Albert, 7
Elizabeth I (queen of
  England), 31, 35
England, 8, 12, 15, 31, 34,
  36, 46, 70
English Heritage, 40
English Revolution, 41
Enigma of Stonehenge, The
  (Fowles), 88
equinox, 81
Europe, 35, 55, 86, 90, 91

Evans, Sir Arthur, 68
Evelyn, John, 40
Exeter, 13

Faerie Quene, The (Spenser),
  30, 31
Fitzpatrick, Andrew, 100
flying saucers, 96
folklore, 31, 34
Fowles, Richard, 88
France, 31
Frankenbury Camp, 96
fraternal orders, 92
freemasons, 92
French, 29

Gale, Roger, 51
Gale, Samuel, 45, 51
Galliard, John, 33
Gaunt, Bonnie, 98
Geoffrey of Monmouth, 26,
  27, 29, 30, 34, 38, 40, 43,
  70, 95
Germany, 43
Giants' Ring, 27, 28, 70, 95
Gladstone, William, 99
Glastonbury, 94
Glastonbury Abbey, 98
Glisson, 40
God, 25, 90, 98, 99, 100
Gowland, William, 66, 67,
  68, 72
graffiti, 72
Great Pyramid, 98
Great Trilithon, 16, 78
Greece, 37, 43, 49, 57, 86
Greek, 23
Grovely Castle, 95, 96

Hades, 34

Hamlet (Shakespeare), 6
Hampshire Avon, 70
Hardy, Thomas, 59
Harrington, Sir John, 35, 44
Harvard University, 79
Hawkins, Gerald, 79, 80, 81,
  82, 83, 85
Hawley, William, 68, 69, 71,
  81, 99, 102
Hayward, Thomas, 57
Hebrews, 55
Heel Stone, 23, 24, 52, 54,
  59, 73, 76, 80, 81, 84, 101
Hengist (Saxon king), 30
Henry of Huntingdon, 8, 26
Henry VII (king of
  England), 30
Hercules, 43
Heyetesbury, 61
History of Great Britain
  (Lewis), 34
History of the Kings of Britain
  (Geoffrey of Monmouth),
  26
Hoare, Richard Colt, 62, 102
holy land, 90
Horatio, 6
Hoyle, Fred, 82, 83, 84

Internet, 102
Ireland, 27, 28, 29, 31, 44,
  95
Irish Sea, 70
Iron Age, 64, 95
Italy, 37, 43

James I (king of England),
  37
James II (king of England),
  48

Jerusalem, 99
Jesus of Nazareth, 55
Jones, Inigo, 37, 38, 39, 41

Kennet River, 45
Kildare, 28
King Arthur, 98

Lambarde, William, 35, 44
Layamon, 29
Leland, John, 30
Lewis, John, 34
leys, 95
Libby, Willard, 71, 72
lithographs, 58
Loch Ness, 6, 11
Lockyear, Sir Norman, 77,
    78, 79, 95, 96
London, 11, 16, 33, 39
Lubbock, Sir John, 64

Making of Stonehenge
    (Castledean), 27, 58, 90
Marlborough, 44, 45
Marlborough Downs, 45
Maughling, Rolo, 94
Mediterranean, 43, 65, 70
megaliths, 12, 13, 84, 86
Merlin, 27, 29, 31, 32, 33, 34,
    44, 95
*Merlin; or, the Devil of
    Stone-Henge* (Galliard),
    33–34
Merlinsburie. *See*
    Marlborough
Michell, John, 96, 97, 98
Middle Ages, 25, 26, 76
Middle East, 17
monument, 11–12
Monumenta Britannica
    (Aubrey), 48

moon, 76
Moore, Henry, 58
mortise-and-tenon system, 15
Moses, 55
*Most Notable Antiquity of
    Great Britain, The* (Jones),
    37
mounds, 20
Mycenae, 65, 70, 73
Mycenaeans. *See* Phoencians,
mystic numbers, 98
myths
    associated with a legend, 34
    described as spiritual center,
        90, 92
    folklore, 31
    human sacrifices, 63
    magical healing power,
        27–28, 99
    a memorial stone, 30
    temple site, 15, 49, 69

National Trust, 66, 90, 92,
    101
    director general of, 90
Neolithic Age, 68
New Age, 87, 88, 89
Newall, R.H., 68, 69
Newdyk, Robert, 37
Newell, R.S., 22
Newham, Peter, 79, 84
New Jerusalem, 98
Noah, 99
Norway, 41
Nunneley, Charles, 102

Office of Works, 68, 92
Old Sarum (medieval town),
    95
Old Sarum Ley, 96
Oxford University, 84

Palladio, 37
pantomime, 33
Pendragon, Uther, 28
Pepys, Samuel, 100
Peter's Mound, 84, 86
Phoenicians, 43, 55, 75
Piggott, Stuart, 26, 70, 71, 72
planets, 76
Pliny, 50
policemen, 91, 93
post holes, 21–22
prehistoric times, 62, 91, 95,
    96, 98
pre-Roman, 65, 79
Preseli Mountain, 70
priest, 29, 49
Puritan, 33
Puritan army, 41
Pythagoras, 49

Queensberry, marquis of, 62,
    65

radioactive material, 72
Rastell, John, 43
Rawle, Sid, 90
Renaissance, 35
Robinson Crusoe (Defoe), 14
Roman Knights, Society of,
    55
Romans, 54, 62, 65, 68, 75
Rome, 37
Rowley, Thomas, 32
Royal Society, 47, 51

sacred numbers, 98
Saint David's Head, 70
Salisbury, 13, 31, 58, 95
Salisbury Cathedral, 13, 96, 98
Sammes, Aylett, 43, 49, 55
sandstone, 15

saracen, 17, 45, 74
sarcen circle, 19, 85
Sasson, Siegfried, 102
Satan, 25, 31, 32
Saxon invaders, 27
scientists, 62, 99, 101
Screeton, Paul, 96
Severn River, 70
Shakespeare, William, 6, 32
Shem, 99
Siculus, Diodorus, 50
Sidbury Hill, 78, 95, 96
Sidney, Sir Philip, 14
skeleton, 63, 100
Slaughter Stone, 23, 59, 62, 74
Smith, John, 57, 76, 95
solar system, 95
solstice, 60, 76, 78, 90, 93
South Pacific, 97
Spain, 43
Spenser, Edmund, 30, 31
Station Stones, 20, 21, 74, 79,
    80, 82, 83
Stone, J.F.S., 71, 72
stone circles, 12, 37, 40, 84, 91
Stonehenge
    facts
        carvings on, 72–73
        donated to government,
        68
        excavations, 66, 69, 72
        former owners, 62, 65, 68
        initiation of Druids, 63
        is a national treasure, 66
        is a stone circle, 13
        location, 11, 13
        meaning of name, 69
        number of stones, 14
        paintings, 58
        restoration work on, 66
        stones as souvenirs, 40

tourist site, 36
various stages of
    construction, 73–75
theories of
    Ancient Britons, 45–46,
    96
    Anglo-Saxons, 43
    Danes, 65
    Druids, 50–57
    magical, 31, 65, 96
    Phoenicians, 43, 65, 73
    Romans, 39, 65
Stonehenge (Atkinson), 69
Stonehenge and Its Mysteries
    (Balfour), 78
Stonehenge Bottom, 75
Stonehenge Complete
    (Chippindale), 14, 16, 30,
    49
Stonehenge Decoded
    (Hawkins), 80
Stonehenge Ley, 96
stone tools, 67
Stukeley, William, 36, 40, 51
    52, 53, 54, 55, 56, 57, 60,
    76, 90, 99
sun, 54, 76
surveyor, 95
Symonds, Richard, 17

Templa Druidium (Aubrey's
    manuscript), 51
*Temple Restor'd to the British
    Druids, A* (Wesley), 56
Tess of the d'Urbervilles
    (Hardy), 59
Thom, Alexander, 84, 86
Thomas, H.H., 69
Thompson, William Irwin, 88
Thomsen, Christian Jurgen,
    62

Thurman, John, 34
Times of London (newspa-
    per), 90
Toland, John, 51
trilithons, 16, 17, 65, 66, 73,
    76, 78, 85
Tripoli, 65
Troy. *See* Mycenae
tunnel, 101
Turkey, 65
Turner, J.M.W., 58

Underwood, Guy, 99

Vergil, Polydore, 30, 34, 43
Viking. *See* Danes
Villers, George (duke of
    Buckingham), 37
Virtimere (Vortigern's son),
    30
Vortigern, 30

Wace, Robert, 29
Wales, 39, 70
Watkins, Alfred, 95
Webb, John, 37, 38, 39, 41,
    42
Wesley, John, 56
Western Europe, 11
White, John B., 80
William of Newburgh, 29
Wilton, 37
Wiltshire, 47, 77, 91
Wood, John, 57
Wordsworth, William, 59
World War I, 68
World War II, 97
Worm, Olaus, 41
Wyle River, 70

Yorkshire, 59

Picture Credits

About the Author

William W. Lace is a native of Fort Worth, Texas. He holds a bachelor's degree from Texas Christian University, a master's degree from East Texas State University, and a doctorate from the University of North Texas. After writing for newspapers in Baytown, Texas, and Fort Worth, he joined the University of Texas at Arlington, eventually becoming director of the News Service. He is now executive assistant to the chancellor at Tarrant County College in Fort Worth. He has written more than twenty books for Lucent, one of which—*The Death Camps* in the Holocaust Library series—was selected by the New York Public Library for its 1999 Recommended Teenage Reading List. He and his wife Laura, a retired school librarian, live in Arlington, Texas, and have two grown children.